	DATE DUE		

Decorative
HANDMADE
PAPER

Decorative

HANDMADE PAPER

JANE MANSFIELD

CHANCELLOR
PRESS

Published in 1996 by Chancellor Press
an imprint of Reed Books Ltd, Michelin House, 81 Fulham Road
London SW3 6RB and Auckland, Melbourne, Singapore and Toronto

By arrangement with Merehurst Limited
Ferry House, 51-57 Lacy Road, Putney, London SW15 1PR
Copyright © Merehurst Limited 1995

ISBN 1 85152 978 0

A catalogue record of this book is available from the British Library.

Edited by **Heather Dewhurst**
Designed by **Lisa Tai**
Photography by **Jon Bouchier**

Typeset by J&L Composition Ltd, Filey, North Yorshire
Colour separation by Global Colour
Printed in Singapore by C. S. Graphics.

Contents

Introduction

Papermaking is a subtle art. Paper is an ephemeral material that we take so much for granted, so accustomed are we to it. Yet it has not always been so. So what is paper?

Paper is derived from the cellulose within plants. This is broken down into individual fibres which have been intentionally damaged so that they will later bond together better. This process is known as 'fibrilation'. These fibres are then re-formed into sheets, whose strength is obtained by the interlocking of the damaged fibres.

If you asked a random sample of people what they thought the earliest paper was made of, a series of misconceptions would be revealed. Many believe that parchment and vellum (sheep and goat or calf skin respectively) are papers, a confusion added to by the paper industry itself by naming certain papers 'parchment'. Papyrus is also commonly considered to be paper; how-ever, this was made from strips of an acquatic weed called *Cyperus papyrus*. These strips were first laid in a grid and pounded, then laminated together into sheets.

When traders from the East brought back drawings and paintings on what looked like paper, our forbears knew that much rice was grown in the Orient and thought that they must therefore be formed from rice. In fact, it was the pith of the plant *Tetrapanx papyrifera* which had been cut into sheets. The edible rice paper used in cooking is usually made from maize and potato starch.

A brief history of papermaking

The first true fibrilated paper was made by T'sai Lun. At 14 years old, he entered service in the Imperial Court of the Han Dynasty as a eunuch and rose through the court, at least in part, because of his working with paper. It was 105AD when he announced his invention to Emperor Ho Ti, and the first sheets were formed of a mixture of old rags, fishing nets, hemp and bark. T'sai Lun continued to improve on his original paper and, within 40 years, paper was the cheapest writing material available in China. Fabrication of the paper was kept a closely guarded secret, but inevitably the information eventually leaked out and the secret of paper-making travelled further west, following the lines of trade, until 1100AD when paper-making commenced in Morocco.

When the Moors conquered Spain, paper-making

▶ *A resurgence of interest in papermaking has led to a wide range of exciting uses for handmade paper.*

followed into Europe around 1150AD. But it was not until the 1480s that papermaking was first practised in Britain, when John Tate set up a mill on the banks of the River Beane near Hertford. By this time, paper currency had been in use in China for some 600 years. A clear divide between Occidental and Oriental papermakers had now arisen in materials used. Papermakers were looking for fibres that remained both long and strong after processing, and had experimented with their local fauna wherever they happened to be worldwide. This resulted in Japanese papermakers traditionally using kozo, gampi and mitsumata; hemp, flax and esparto grass were favoured elsewhere, but in Europe, cotton and linen rags became the main source.

The mills were all located next to rivers for their clean water and power source, and tended if possible to be close to the populated areas for their supply of rags. The exact methods for processing the raw materials would vary from mill to mill and from time to time but, basically, rags were taken to the mills for sorting,

where buttons, hooks-and-eyes, etc, were first removed. Then the sorted rags were rotted, either by leaving them in damp piles to ferment or, less desirable for the final paper, lime was spread on them to speed the rotting. There was a high degree of disease associated with rag handlers, who were usually women and children. The rotted rags were then washed and/or cooked, then placed for pounding under a long line of huge wooden hammers which were raised and dropped by water power on the rags for some three days continuously. Water from the river ran over the rags for the first day in an attempt to cleanse them, but this was a wasteful process because of the many finer fibres that escaped through the sieves that the water passed through before rejoining the river.

A GROWING INDUSTRY

The demand for paper expanded rapidly in the early part of the 17th century. The first newspaper in Britain was printed in London in 1622; the usage of paper as a wall covering was introduced from the Orient; and the general growth in literacy with its consequential call for more and more paper led to a shortage. In 1666 things were so dire in Britain that a decree was passed by Parliament during the reign of Charles II, prohibiting the use of cotton and linen shrouds for burying the dead – only wool was allowed.

By the late 1600s, the search for other suitable papermaking materials was on. In 1719 Réamur, a French naturalist and physicist, recorded that he felt it should be possible to make paper from trees, having observed wasps building their nests.

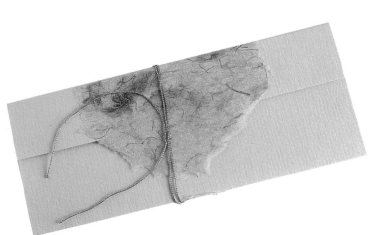

In 1772, Joseph Schäffer produced pamphlets that included paper samples made from various plant fibres, such as potatoes, cabbage stalks and thistles, with only 20 per cent rag input. In 1800, Mathias Koops made paper from both pure straw and wood. The shortage continued, however, and even in 1818, in Britain, it was a punishable offence to publish a newspaper larger than 55 × 80cm (22 × 32in). Eventually, in 1851, 100 per cent wood pulp paper was available.

In the USA, papermakers were exempt from military service during the Civil War, so vital was their role. At that time, in 1863, to combat the shortage of rags in America (still at that stage the main source of paper), a papermaker named Augustus Stamford is reputed to have imported Egyptian mummies for the sole purpose of converting the swathings of the mummies to wrapping paper!

MECHANIZATION

Meanwhile, mechanization of the papermaking industry was under way. It was a French inventor, Nicholas Louis Robert, who first began experi-

menting with a papermaking machine as he wished to get away from the arguments of those involved with papermaking! He took out the first patent in 1798. In 1806 Henry Fourdrinier patented the first forming of continuous sheets of paper by machine, the prototype of today's papermaking machines. Progress continued from then so that the availability of a suitable bulk papermaking material and the mechanization of the papermaking process occurred more or less together. Thus, by the 1870s the making of 100 per cent wood pulp paper in volume on fully automated machines was becoming the norm, leaving low volume 'specialist' papers to be made by hand.

The decline in the number of hand papermakers has continued consistently until relatively recently, when mainly artists have turned back to this source due to their dissatisfaction with mechanically produced papers.

The vast papermaking industry of today now spreads across much of the globe, often processing the wood from one continent into paper in another and it bears little resemblance to the small-scale production of its origin. During its time, paper has been made into products as diverse as coffins, cloth, currency, building materials, unwanted mail shots and vast quantities of toilet tissue; and yet, diversely, it also feeds the computers of today.

I have found something both restful and timeless in the sound of the dripping water and the rhythm of the papermaking process. I trust that you too will experience a part of that delight when you become a link in the chain that leads through time.

Equipment and Materials

Most of the equipment that you will need to start papermaking is probably already in your home, the likely exception being the mould and deckle, which are neither expensive nor difficult to make. So steam on in the knowledge that the most wonderful effects can be achieved using the most primitive equipment.

Basic equipment

PAPERMAKING IS A WET BUSINESS, SO YOU NEED TO work where water can drain away. You also need enough space for your tank, felts, sheets and wet pulp. Once you have established these requirements, you can turn to the more specific materials listed below.

TANK/VAT
You will need a tank/vat to hold the mix of water and fibres from which the paper is made. The size of the largest sheet of paper that you will be able to make will be determined by the wooden frames that you have. These in their turn, should fit comfortably into your tank/vat when being

held firmly by your hands, one on either side. A4 is a bit tight in most washing-up bowls, but a baby bath or an undrilled garden planter which are available in larger sizes do the job nicely. Failing that, you could work directly into a sink, but be careful not to allow too much pulp to go down the drain . . . especially if you have a drainage problem.

THE WOODEN FRAMES – 'MOULD AND DECKLE'
A sheet of paper is made on a wooden frame called a mould. The deckle is the removable wooden frame that sits on the mould to define the paper edge. Making the mould and deckle is

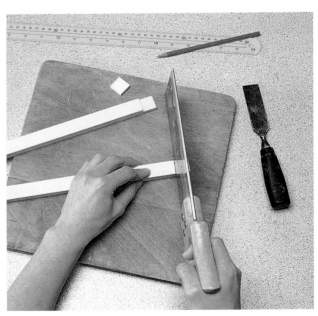

▲ *To make a mould and deckle, saw halfway through the depth of both ends of the eight pieces of wood and chisel out the end pieces.*

▶ *Place the two frames together and drill two holes through each of the overlapping corner pieces. Glue the wood together and secure with screws.*

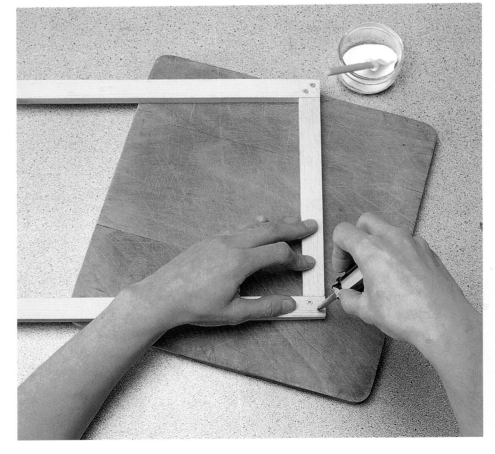

the most fiddly and least rewarding part of paper-making, but it is worth taking some time over, and with care, your mould and deckle could last you many years. (It is possible to buy a mould and deckle ready made, often in papermaking kits. If you would rather buy one, make sure that the mesh is tight.)

Small sheets of paper are easier to make, and use less pulp, so I recommend starting on A5 (148 × 210mm), certainly no larger than A4 (210 × 297mm). Many of the projects in this book could be achieved using an A4 mould, but check that your intended mould and deckle size fits comfortably into your intended vat, with sufficient space for your hands. You may be fortunate enough to find two strong wooden picture frames securely pinned at their corners, in which case just oil or

varnish them as described below. Alternatively you may need to make them yourself.

Making a mould and deckle To make a set you will need a saw, a ruler, a pen/pencil, screws, waterproof wood glue, a hammer and a chisel. Hard wood is preferable for the job, but it is more expensive and soft wood would suffice. Choose a section of wood measuring approximately 1.5 × 1.5cm ($\frac{5}{8}$ × $\frac{5}{8}$in); I find the maximum I can comfortably hold is 2.5cm × 12mm (1 × $\frac{1}{2}$in). Bear in mind that whichever section you choose it should feel comfortable in your hands when you have two pieces, one on top of the other. The most secure yet simple joint to make is a halving joint; to do this you will need to cut the wood allowing for the joining of that piece to two others, top and bottom, so, for a complete mould and deckle set you will need:

> 4 pieces of wood at the length of your sheet plus 2 wood widths
> 4 pieces of wood at the width of your sheet plus 2 wood widths

Mark a line at both ends showing the width of the wood. Saw halfway through the depth of the wood at the line at both ends. Using a hammer and chisel, chisel downwards at the end until a 'bite' has come out. Pare off any wood that will prevent a good union. Do this to each of your eight pieces of wood.

Place together the two frames. Drill two holes through the overlapping corner pieces to about three-quarters of their total depth. Glue the wood together and secure the joints by screwing in screws of the correct length (three-quarters of the total wood depth). Let the glue dry, then apply two coats of wood oil or polyurethane varnish and allow it to dry thoroughly. Leave one frame as it is – this is the deckle.

For the mould you will need some net curtain or wire. If using net, a fairly open gauge nylon/terylene net with no obvious pattern is preferable.

▼ *Attach the net to the mould with drawing pins around each side of the frame, keeping the net taut. Cut off the spare net.*

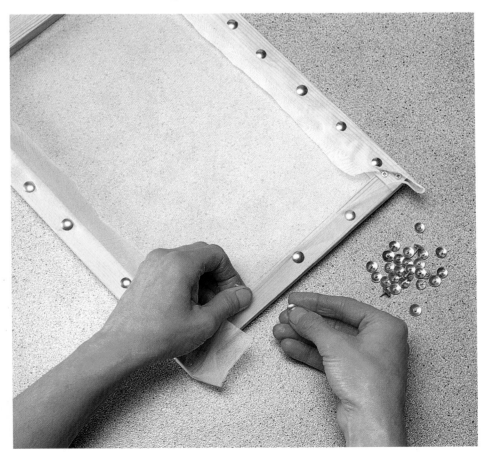

Wire is more difficult to obtain and to handle, but it is harder wearing and on larger sizes it is easier to form sheets of even thickness. You need a wire that will not rust, for example stainless steel, aluminium, or a plastic-coated mild steel wire with 18–22 wires per inch. If you intend to make a mould and deckle for larger sheets than A4, you will definitely need a wire mesh.

Cut the net/wire at least 10cm (4in) larger in both directions than your mould size. Lay the net/wire onto a flat surface and place the mould on top. Attach the net/wire securely to one long side of the mould by inserting drawing pins or staples into the uppermost surface, keeping the net/wire taut on that side. The net will stretch when it is wet, so from now on pull it as tight as you can, without ripping it! The wire, too, needs to be taut. Now secure the opposite edge, starting at the centre. Finally, secure the two remaining short ends. Cut off the spare net/wire. To prevent paper fibres from lodging under the loose edge where it is difficult to clean, you may if you wish tape down the loose edge with brown parcel tape (in the process you will cover the drawing pins/staples). Overtape the corners. Do not get any tape onto the area that will be forming the sheet.

OLD BLANKETS/'FELTS'

These are needed for couching the newly made sheets of paper. Old blankets, towels or nappies need to be cut into pieces approximately 10cm (4in) larger than the largest sheet you intend to make (they can be folded for smaller sheets). If you do not have any of the above, I have seen newspaper wads do a reasonably efficient job. The more felts you have, the greater the pile of papers you will be able to make at a time without having to stop – but you will need at least 12 to get started.

BOARDS

To carry and press your wet pieces of paper, you will need two wooden boards. Ideally, they should be slightly larger than your felts – say an extra 2.5cm (1in) in each direction – but any flat piece of wood larger than your felt will do.

VISCOSE CLOTHS/NAPPY LINERS

Traditionally papermakers worked directly onto felts, but when working with various dyes it is much easier if you protect your felts. It is also easier to get rid of any mistakes from these smooth surfaces than that of a felt. Nappy liners are fine for small sheet sizes, and have the advantage of being transparent, but they do not wear too well. Viscose kitchen cloths with small orange, blue or green square patterns running in diagonals across them wear well and will accommodate up to A4 in size. (Don't buy similar products with diamond patterns and small holes in them – they are not as effective.) If you go any larger than A4, plain cotton or polycotton mixes do the job, but be careful of fraying edges.

LIQUIDIZER

A kitchen liquidizer is extremely useful for making paper pulp. Food processors do not seem to beat the pulp up as quickly or quite as thoroughly, but they do a satisfactory job. Alternatively, you are looking at a bucket and a potato masher, aided in later stages by a food mixer.

PULP INGREDIENTS

Old envelopes, drawings, drawing paper, bills, wrapping paper, paper bags and computer print-out paper are all ideal ingredients for pulp. You could also try flimsier materials, such as egg cartons, tissues, and kitchen towels. The quality of what you put in will be reflected in what you get out and, for this reason, I avoid using newsprint and glossy magazines. The former makes everything filthy and the latter contains very little paper fibre, being mostly comprised of china clay which is responsible for its glossy smooth surface. You may prefer to work with only clean paper and add colouring elements of your choice, for you will find that even a small amount of print on your original paper is enough to tint the whole batch.

Pulp colouring agents

To alter the colour of your pulp, experiment by adding powdered or liquid tempera colours and acrylics, cold water dyes, and even different concentrations of tea and coffee.

Size

It is sometimes necessary to size the paper to give it a coating which prevents it absorbing ink like blotting paper. The simplest sizes to use are wallpaper paste and PVA glue (see page 33).

Plant material

If you are making pure plant paper, you will need plant material that is fibrous but not woody, such as stinging nettles, iris, bamboo leaves, straw and reeds. (See page 36 for how to make pulp from plant material.)

Cotton linters

Use these as an alternative to recycled papers for making pulp. They come in large, thick, slightly creamy coloured sheets and are comprised of fibres from the cotton plant left after the ginning operation. Paper made from cotton linters is soft and much stronger than recycled wood paper; however, the drawback is that cotton linters can be difficult to obtain.

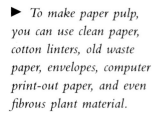

▶ *To make paper pulp, you can use clean paper, cotton linters, old waste paper, envelopes, computer print-out paper, and even fibrous plant material.*

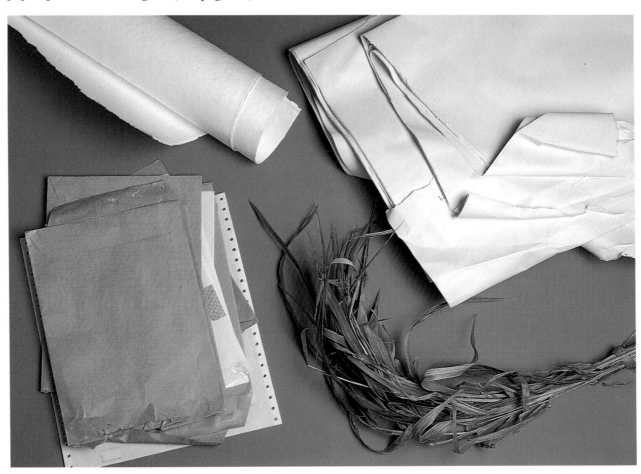

Techniques

The basic techniques of papermaking – from preparing the pulp and making the sheets, to pressing and drying the newly-formed paper – are not difficult to grasp and, once equipped with them, you will have a whole new range of texture at your fingertips. These, when combined with differing colouring agents, will result in a far broader range of papers than is available commercially.

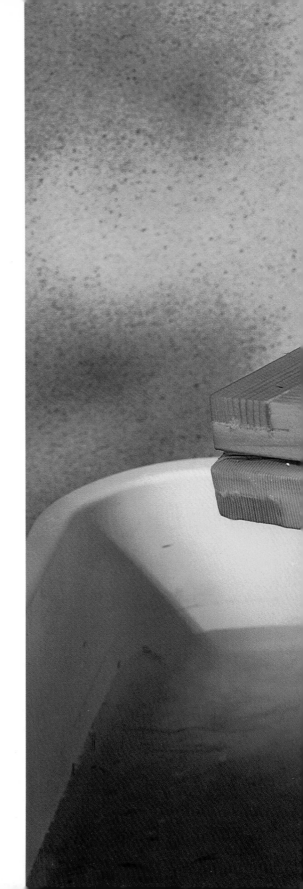

Basic techniques

THERE ARE SEVERAL ADVANTAGES TO A BEGINNER TO papermaking of using a recycled paper base, namely its availability, relative cheapness and ease of preparation. The traditional method of preparing the pulp described below, however, holds good for other pulps, for example cotton linters or pure plant – though each pulp prepared from different·sources will have slightly different characteristics to work with.

A word of warning before you begin – papermaking is a wet business; both you and the surfaces that you work on, including the floor, are likely to get, at the least, splashed. So it is advisable to wear an apron and protect your surfaces with plastic sheeting.

PREPARING THE PULP

Tear the pieces of your chosen paper into 2.5–5cm (1–2in) squares. Leave to soak overnight in cold water. If you are in a hurry, soak the pieces in hot water for as long as you can, so that the paper is wet all the way through. Just one bucket of torn paper (prior to the wetting, and consequent

compacting taking place), will probably be ample to start with.

Place the soaked pieces of paper into a liquidizer goblet to a capacity of approximately one-eighth to one-quarter full. Do not compact them or press them down. Cover with warm water so the goblet is approximately two-thirds full. Process the paper until it is completely broken down. If you hear the liquidizer motor straining, switch it off and reload, as some paper has probably stuck on the blades.

To test whether the paper has completely broken down, put a tablespoon of ground-up pulp from the liquidizer goblet into a jam jar of water. Stir it thoroughly and then hold the jam jar up to the light. If you can see small pieces of paper floating in it, return it to the blender and process again. The pulp is ready when there are no paper pieces remaining in the liquid.

If you do not possess a liquidizer, you will have to soak the paper as before. Then, using a potato masher, pound it up and down in the wet paper. After you have broken the paper up roughly with

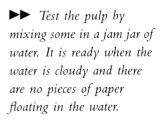

▶ *Place pieces of soaked paper into a liquidizer goblet so that it is approximately one-eighth to one-quarter full.*

▶▶ *Test the pulp by mixing some in a jam jar of water. It is ready when the water is cloudy and there are no pieces of paper floating in the water.*

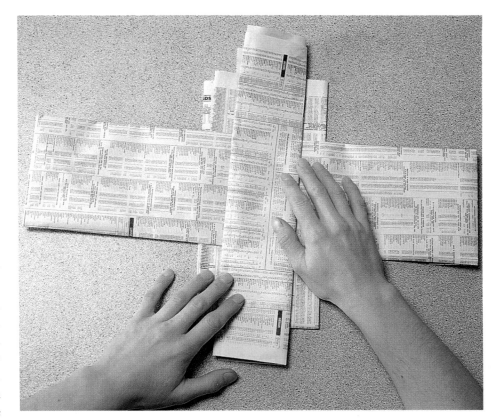

the potato masher, use a kitchen mixer to mix the paper for approximately ten minutes. You will probably not achieve a completely broken-down pulp (especially if you are using a potato masher alone), but you will still be able to achieve a pleasing result.

After preparing the pulp, fill your vat to a depth of approximately 10cm (4in) with hand-hot water. Add the pulped paper. Initially you will probably need two to three liquidizer loads. You are aiming for a broth-like consistency; at the thickest it should feel like thin custard and definitely not thick porridge! If you have added too much pulp, scoop it out with a sieve, and add later as required.

Put down one of your boards next to the vat in a landscape position, and form a cross from folded newspaper on top of it. Fold another sheet to a narrower width and place it front to back on top of the cross. Place three damp felts on top of this. Prepare and have close to hand a bucket of warm water in which to dampen and squeeze out the viscose cloths. You are now ready to make your first sheet.

FORMING THE SHEET

Agitate the water in the vat and mix the pulp thoroughly with your hands to ensure that all fibres are evenly distributed through the water. Place the deckle (the open frame) on the mould (the netted frame), with the netted surface sandwiched in the middle. Hold the mould and deckle together firmly at their sides.

Slide the mould and deckle into the water, and down to the bottom of the vat. Then slide them back along the bottom of the vat and upwards out of the water keeping them level. (There is a suction as you bring the mould and deckle out of the water.) Immediately, while there is water on the mould, shake it forwards and backwards and from side to side. Forming a sheet is more effective when it is done with clear unhesitating

movements; try to perform the dipping in of the mould and deckle and the shaking as if they were one action.

Stop shaking the mould and deckle before the water has drained away completely. You only have a couple of seconds to do the shaking; its purpose is to bind the fibres that form the sheet together and thus make a stronger sheet. If you do not shake the mould and deckle, you will probably have sheets of even thickness straight away, but do not let a few uneven sheets at the start put you off; it will not take long to get the hang of it. Rest the mould and deckle on the side of the vat.

Take a viscose cloth and wet it in a bucket of warm water. Squeeze it out as hard as you can, so that it is just damp. Open it up, shake it to get rid of any creases and place it onto the pile of felts on the board, allowing any spare cloth to hang over the front.

▲ *To make a post, form a cross from folded newspaper. Then lay another narrower folded sheet on top, going from front to back.*

Tip the mould and deckle with one corner pointing towards the vat to encourage any excess moisture to drain from the sheet. Lift off the deckle and place it on one side, taking care not to damage the sheet. Invert the mould with the newly formed sheet onto the dampened cloth. (Do not worry, it should not fall off.) Press firmly on all of the outer edges and immediately hold the viscose cloth down with one hand and peel back the mould smoothly and quickly from the side at which you are holding the cloth.

Cover the sheet with the spare half of the viscose cloth or another dampened uncreased cloth. Should you get any creases in your cloth when you place it onto the wet sheet, lift the cloth and stretch the crease out before replacing it on the sheet as any creases will be marked in the surface of your sheet forever.

To make a new sheet, you will need a new damp felt and dampened cloth to be placed on top of the last covered sheet. More pulp will need to be added every sheet or so, depending on sheet thickness and size. The warm water from the vat can be used to mix up new pulp in the liquidizer. Keep topping the vat up with hot water as necessary, depending on the warmth and depth of the water.

If you have made a sheet that you have over-shaken, or do not like for some reason, remove the deckle and invert the mould with the sheet, so that it touches the surface of the water. The sheet will then come off. Similarly, if you make a mistake while couching (putting your newly made sheet onto the cloths), simply pick the cloth up and touch it onto the surface of the water and the sheet will come off. In both instances you will need to agitate the pulp/water

▲ *To make a sheet, agitate the vat of pulp then slide the mould and deckle into the water and down to the bottom of the vat.*

▶ *In one continuous movement, slide the mould and deckle upwards out of the water, keeping them level. Shake the mould forwards and backwards and from side to side.*

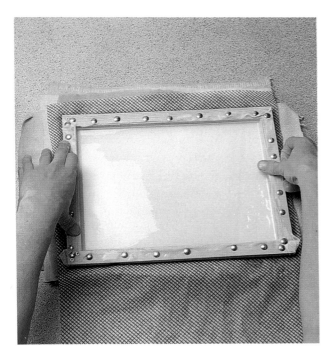

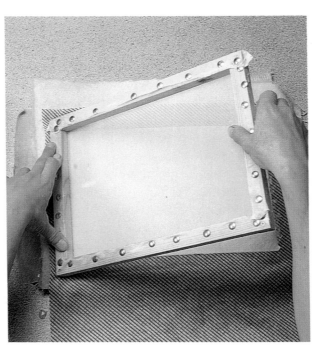

◀◀ *After the water has drained away, lift the deckle off the mould and invert the mould onto a dampened cloth.*

◀ *Press firmly on all outer edges of the mould and then peel back the mould smoothly and quickly.*

▼ *If you make a mistake when forming a sheet, remove the deckle and invert the mould into the vat. The sheet will then come off.*

mix extra well before proceeding to make the next sheet.

When you have made enough sheets of paper, or run out of viscose cloths, and can continue no further, place a final felt on top of the last viscose cloth-covered sheet and put your second board on top of that.

After finishing papermaking, wash your equipment thoroughly, in particular removing any fibres that are on the mould. A nail brush and running water are helpful, but inevitably some fibres will be stuck underneath the net or wire on the wood of the mould. Do not worry about these but, if possible, remove them at the edge, so that they do not prevent drainage through the mesh. Leave cloths and felts where they will dry properly, and if you have been using a plant, or other dye that has stained the cloths, wash these well before drying and storing them – if necessary using a mild bleach solution before washing. Dry the excess moisture from your mould and deckle and store them underneath a weighted board to prevent them warping.

STORING UNUSED PULP

Pulp, when left standing for a couple of days in warm conditions, will soon become slimy and smelly. You may find that you wish to store excess pulp for later use. Drain off the excess water through a sieve. The remaining pulp will keep for a couple of days in a refrigerator, but if you need to store it for longer you will need to freeze or dry it. Dry the pulp by hanging it in a muslin or net bag in a warm place – if you are contemplating storing pulp that contains plants or a non-dye-fast fibre, be aware that its colour may fade from its original shade, possibly at the expense of dyeing the surrounding pulp.

▶ *An effective way of pressing sheets is to place a pile of them on the floor, sandwiched between two boards, and then stand on them.*

▶ *If you have an old metal press, place the pile of sheets in the press and screw the press down tightly.*

▶▶ *When couching a sheet, lift the viscose cloth that the sheet is laid on, onto a board with a single felt. Let the cloth and sheet sag in the centre.*

PRESSING THE SHEETS

The surface texture of your sheet will depend largely upon the method of drying and pressing that you select. Conventionally sheets are pressed, air dried and then re-pressed using many tons of pressure. But there are ways around this. For all of the following methods (except drying on a weighted cloth, when no pressing is necessary), you will first need to press the excess moisture from your sheets. You may expect, subject to the number and size of sheets made, to produce a river of water; for this operation, the garden or garage may be best suited. In all cases, continue to apply pressure until the water from the pile of papers has slowed to a drip. The drier that you can get your papers, the easier they will be to handle, as very wet sheets tend to stretch or tear when held unsupported.

Standing Place the pile of papers in their sandwiching boards on the floor and stand on it – squeeze a friend on with you if any are available!

Old press You may be fortunate enough to have access to an old metal press. Screw the press down onto the pile of papers as tightly as possible.

Car jack press If you do not have a press, a car jack is the next best thing, and is especially worth considering if you are making a larger batch of paper when drying space may be short. Place your

.papers under one of the jacking points – the end with the engine is best as it is heaviest. Position the jack between the jacking point and the centre of the top board. Jack up until the vehicle is just off the ground – nothing is to be gained by going any higher.

Flower press Most flower presses that I have seen are too small to be of much use, and they provide little pressure. However, if you intend to use one, beware of getting it wet . . . it may warp and the screws may rust.

If you intend to dry your sheet on a window or other smooth surface, I would leave it at one pressing, but if you find that your sheets are too wet to handle safely, you may either (a) repeat the above procedure, having first formed a new interleafing of sheets in their viscose cloths with any spare dry felts or newpapers that you may have, or (b) add an extra stage to the making of future sheets that will probably mean that you only need one pressing. Couch your sheet as usual, but do not leave the board at the bottom of the pile (you will still need the newspaper camber under the felts). Instead, place the board with one felt on it next to the couching area. Each time that you couch a sheet, lift the viscose cloth that the sheet is on, onto the board with the single felt. Allow the cloth and the sheet to sag at the centre as you carry it. You must try to align the sheets as accurately as possible, otherwise the sheets will receive uneven pressure, which may result in an uneven layer. When the pile is as large as you want it to be, put on a top felt, then board and press it as usual. This method is also very useful if you have access to a spin dryer or a mangle and have only a limited supply of felts, enabling you to make more sheets for pressing in one go than you would otherwise.

If you are going to be making several different shapes or sizes of paper at one go, it will be worth separating each shape or size on a different felt-covered board. In that way a multi-storey sandwich of boards and papers can be pressed at once, so giving all of the sheets an even pressure.

DRYING

The method of drying you decide upon will also help determine the look of the finished paper.

Conventional air drying and re-pressing This results in a potentially smooth sheet on both surfaces, but it is dependent for a smooth finish on prolonged exposure to a lot of pressure. By using a car jack for pressure, you should be able to write on the dry sheet, but if you are only using a

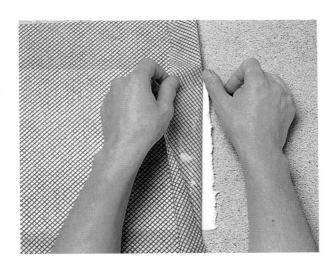

◀ *To remove the viscose cloth, peel it back until an edge of the sheet is visible. Brush downwards on the edge of the sheet with your thumb.*

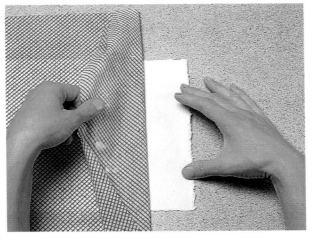

◀ *The sheet will start to come off the cloth. Hold down the loosened sheet and peel back the cloth with your other hand.*

book for pressure, your finished sheet will have a textured surface.

Unpack the pile of papers until you come to the first sheet in its viscose cloth. Open the cloth up. Invert it onto a clean dry surface where it is to dry and peel back the edge of the cloth until an edge of the sheet, preferably a narrow one, is visible. Brush downwards on the edge of your sheet with a finger or thumb, and the sheet should start to come off the cloth. Hold down the loosened sheet and peel back the cloth with your other hand. As the sheets dry, they will curl up at the edges; do not put them anywhere too hot, as the faster they dry, the more they will curl and the harder they will be to flatten later.

When dry, either interleave the dry sheets between magazines and place them between boards under the jacked-up car and leave overnight, or place them between the pages of a heavy book and leave them for as long as possible and/or until you need to use them. (If using a book to press, make especially sure that the sheets are bone dry before inserting them.)

▼ *As sheets dry they curl up a little at the edges. If they dry too quickly they will curl up more and it will be harder to flatten them later.*

▲ *To keep a sheet flat while it is drying, invert the sheet onto a damp cloth, then peg the cloth to the edges of a board and leave to dry.*

On a weighted cloth This is suitable if you are not making lots of sheets, and if drying over a couple of days or longer will not be a problem. Simply make the sheet, invert it onto a damp cloth and remove both sheet and cloth to the drying location. Bricks can be used to weight down the edges of a sheet or, by drying on a board, you can peg the cloth to the board edges. Drying in a closed cloth will result in two cloth-like surfaces or opening up a cloth (which will speed drying slightly) will result in one cloth-like and one rough surface. When the sheet is properly dry, peel it off and it is ready for use. Pressing out excess water before drying would result in a more compact sheet and speedier drying.

Ironing Unpack the pile of papers until you come to the cloth-covered sheet, and peel the sheet off. Ironing directly onto the surface of the paper will result in a polished effect (rather like that on the seat of a pair of well-worn trousers), and you may prefer to iron it dry between a tea-towel, or a piece of tissue, cartridge or blotting paper.

Do not iron directly onto a piece of paper containing petals or other fragile plant fragments, as the heat of the iron may destroy their colour and damage them.

Drying under pressure This is a labour-intensive method of drying, but it gives the sheet a slightly grainy but flat finish on both sides. Unpack the pile of papers and felts, leaving the sheets in their viscose cloths. Form a new interleaving of dry felts/blotting paper and sheets between two, preferably dry, outer boards. Leave under pressure (the jacked-up car, the old press or a large pile of bricks, etc). Change felts at approximately two-hourly intervals until real wetness has gone and then every 12 hours or so until completely dry. Depending upon how wet the sheets were to start with, it should take approximately six to seven changes for them to dry, but do not take them out and unpeel them from their cloth until they are quite dry as they will curl even if only slightly damp.

Photographer's old glazing plate or heating press These are not easy to come by, but you never know what lurks in attics. These old presses produce surfaces flat enough to write on, even though slightly mottled in texture, but

beware of using sheets with fragile petals or other plant material in them as the heat may damage the petals. Simply peel the wet sheet from its cloth, place on the heated plate, put the lid down and wait until it is dry.

On a windowpane The side that is to be dried in contact with the glass is going to be very smooth. It is easiest to keep the sheet supported on the cloth as described below, which will result in the wire side (under-surface when you make it) being smooth. If you wish the felt side (uppermost surface when you make it) to be smooth, you will need first to take it off the cloth and then carefully stick it to the glass. Unpack the sheets and open up the viscose cloth. Wipe the window with a wet cloth so that the window becomes wet. Lift the cloth with the wet sheet on it to the windowpane. Through the cloth, press the sheet onto the glass, using a pad of some sort for even pressure (for example, a screwed-up cloth), and brush from the centre outwards. When you are sure that the sheet is sticking, let it go, and peel off the cloth. You may at this stage roll it very carefully with a rolling pin so that the sheet is pressed to the glass as firmly as possible. Leave it for a few days until you are sure that it is completely dry and

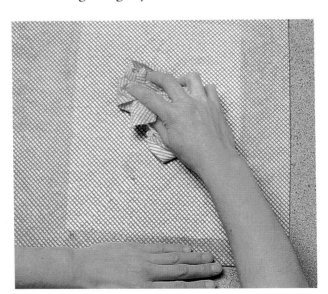

◄◄ *To dry a sheet on glass, wet the glass then place the cloth with the wet sheet on it on the glass. Press the sheet to the glass through the cloth.*

◄ *When you are sure that the sheet is sticking to the glass, let it go and peel off the cloth.*

then carefully peel the sheet off the glass.

Paper will 'take' any surface that it dries against, so the same method may be used on wood to give a wooden grain finish. Experiment with other surfaces; there are many effects available.

Sheets made from cotton linters do not always remain in position against glass while they are drying; where they detach themselves they can warp, as with air drying.

NB: Newly-made sheets, especially those made by conventional air drying and re-pressing, may be prone to slight upward curling of the edges. To remedy this, after they are dry, place the sheets in a pile, and do not leave them anywhere too dry, too damp or too hot. Flip through your pile each day or so, re-arrange their order and they will soon settle down. Conventionally, sheets are left for three months to stabilize before being considered to be saleable.

WATERMARKING

This is not, as you may have expected, achieved with the aid of water. A simple watermark is fairly easy to achieve and, with a good design, can be very effective in a thinner sheet and add a personal touch to your paper – the effect is lost in medium to heavyweight sheets. It is worth bearing in mind that you may not find them desirable in all situations, for example unless specifically designed for the purpose I do not personally like them displayed against a strong light source in sheets incorporating free flowing plants.

Their effect is achieved by raising and depressing the mould surface, thus resulting in thinner and thicker sheets at those points. Depressing the mould surface is difficult unless you have a wire mould screen and special equipment (the making of watermarks is a complete trade unto itself within the paper industry). However, raising the mould surface is not hard to do, and watermarks can be achieved in four ways.

Multi-purpose adhesives The fastest method, which tends to work best with bold designs, is to draw your design using general-purpose glue directly onto the mould mesh. Where the glue is applied, the paper will be thinner when it is

▲ *Watermark patterns are created by raising the mould surface, using adhesives, art masking fluid, wire or cotton.*

Art masking fluid This is thin enough to be applied with a paintbrush or stylus, and can give a much more flowing and detailed result than the sticky glues applied direct from the tube. Art masking fluid is also fast to apply and ready to use very quickly, but you cannot build up the effect as you can with thicker glues. It works simply by blocking the drainage holes in the mesh of the mould and thus alters the settling patterns of the paper fibres. Lines should not be wider than 3mm ($\frac{1}{8}$in).

Over time, both of these first two methods of watermarking will deteriorate, but they are both very simple to touch-up or remove completely when no longer wanted. To remove them from the mould surface, gently pick and rub the design off with your fingers or, if necessary, use the appropriate solvent.

The wire method This method is how the earliest watermarks were achieved. You simply bend a piece of non-rusting wire (approximately 1mm ($\frac{1}{16}$in) thick, into the desired shape of your design with a pair of long-nosed pliers, and then tack the finished design into place on the mould surface with cotton, waxed cotton or fine fishing thread (the fine tacking stitches will be barely visible in the watermark).

Sewing Any design may be sewn onto the mould surface to act as a watermarking device. Although it takes longer to execute than the gluing or wire method, it will potentially give you fine detail similar to that achieved using art masking fluid. Any strong thread may be used. I like working with fine fishing line, but cotton or waxed cotton are fine (for a longer lasting cotton, run a candle along your piece of cotton a few times to waterproof it before you start to work). Always tie on and off on the reverse side of the mould. Different depths can be achieved by building up your design to varying heights: but be careful not to go too high or you will break through the surface of the sheet and leave a hole.

▲ *The resulting watermarked sheet shows how you can achieve more or less detail using different methods of watermarking.*

made. You can build up the design further by waiting for the glue to dry and applying more glue. If you prefer, and you have a net mesh on your mould, you can first draw or trace the design. When the glue is dry, the mould is ready for use.

ALTERNATIVE METHODS OF FORMING SHEETS

There are few hard and fast rules in papermaking, and there are many different means of achieving your own ends – experiment with combinations of the following techniques. The first sheets made in China were, for instance, probably poured into a mould suspended in a stream. The next method is a variation of this.

Pouring sheets This will produce sheets of differing densities. Each pulp will retain water differently, and so determine how far the fibres will spread from where you pour them before they settle. This may be done with or without a deckle depending on whether you wish to have a straight or wiggly edge. Pre-mix sufficient pulp and water to cover the whole mould. Very thin sheets are difficult to remove intact so, initially, I would recommend that you make the mix thick enough so that when poured you do not see the mesh clearly. Later you can go onto very thin or holey sheets, but then, do not apply any surface coatings (such as PVA) to the sheet while still on the mould which might make the paper stick at the holey edges!

Tip your pulp and water mix into something that will pour better, for example a jug. Place the mould (and if desired the deckle), supported in a flat position over a sink or similar area to allow water to pass through. Pour the pulp directly onto the mould. You may use any pattern of pouring that you choose, which should be visible on the finished sheet. If you wish to manipulate the pulp at all by hand, a paint scraper or an artist's paint trowel are useful. I would usually recommend mould drying after pouring a sheet, so that none of the 'character' achieved by pouring is lost.

Mould drying Any sheet can be mould dried. The result will be a distinctive surface on the upper side of the sheet as it has never been flattened in any way, and the wire pattern on the underside. The disadvantage is the length of time that sheets take to dry. It may be a suitable method, therefore, to experiment with on the last sheet each time you have your equipment out. Leave the mould flat until it stops dripping completely, which may be an hour or so. Large sheets will take considerably longer to stop dripping.

Remove the deckle (if used) and then stand the

▶ *To make a poured sheet, suspend the mould over a bowl and slowly pour the pulp from a jug directly onto the mould.*

▶ *If you leave a sheet to drain in one direction only it may take on a 'crying' appearance. To avoid this, rotate it regularly while it is drying.*

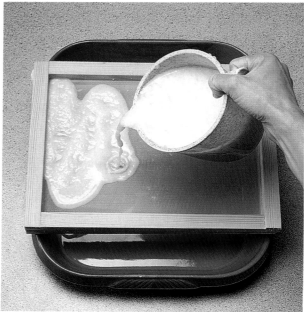

mould on end preferably in a warm place, or in a good draught where the air can circulate around both faces of the mould. A radiator could be useful (but protect the flooring if necessary as the sheet may start to drip slightly when stood upright). On a sunny day you may leave the mould against an outside window or on the covered floor with the sheet facing towards the glass or the wall so that no insects or dust adhere to the surface of the wet sheet. Put a brick or similar weight on the mould bottom to prevent it being blown in the wind.

If you have a mesh open enough for the fibres to get through, you may find that the paper sinks into the mesh while it dries. This makes successful removal difficult, so do not leave the mould to lie on its back to dry for any longer than is necessary after it has stopped dripping. Also beware if you are using plants that bleed colour into the surrounding paper, or other means of colouring that may also bleed while drying. You will find that the sheet may take on a 'crying' appearance as the colour bleeds in one direction only. To rectify this, you will initially need to sponge excess moisture from the sheet by gently drawing out water through the back of the mould and then rotate it regularly while drying. To remove the dry sheet from the mould, loosen an edge with your finger or a blunt knife and gently peel it off. If you have a net mesh, you should be able to push the net away from the paper for ease of removal.

Laminating To stick two or more wet sheets together, make a sheet as usual and put it out onto the viscose cloth. Make a second sheet and put it directly onto the first. Repeat as desired. Cover, press and dry as usual.

To sandwich objects between sheets, make a sheet as usual and lay desired objects (preferably flattish) onto the surface of the laid-down sheet. Make a second sheet and lay it directly onto the first. Cover, press and dry as usual. You may care to do this with very thin sheets (possibly without a

▲ *To sandwich objects between sheets, lay flattish objects onto a newly formed sheet. Lay a second sheet directly on top.*

◄ *To add a coloured pattern to a sheet, make the first sheet as usual. Then pour a second coloured sheet in a swirly pattern and lay it directly onto the first.*

deckle), thus making the encapsulated pieces visible when the sheet is held up to the light.

In both instances you will need to be careful of air bubbles forming in the sheets as the cloths and felts that you are working on become saturated with water. To reduce the risk, ensure that the sheets have dripped off as much excess moisture as possible before pressing onto the cloth, and lift the viscose cloth with the first sheet to one side for a moment, allowing the sheet to bend slightly in the centre while carrying. Place another damp felt on top of the pile, replace the sheet and add extra lamination. Repeat this procedure for each additional layer.

Laying items on the mould Anything that may be laid on the mould surface while the sheet is formed will have two effects: the first is that of preventing pulp settling where the obstruction is, and the second is that of leaving a deckled edge at the edge of the obstruction. Ideally the items will have enough self-weight to stay in place while you make the sheet. If not, you will have to hold or weight the item in place (small kitchen weights are very useful for this). Remove the items before couching the sheet.

If the item and the space that it leaves are more than 1–2cm ($\frac{1}{2}$–$\frac{3}{4}$in) wide, you may find that you need to simulate the effect of the mould pressing along the inner edge of the resulting hole with your finger. You may also have to take extra care while removing the sheet from the viscose cloth and brush off extra 'edges' as they are revealed in the sheet.

DECKLED EDGE

The wavy irregular edge that you get on a piece of handmade paper formed in one sheet is, I think, an intrinsic part of the feel. You may wish at some stage to control the edge by accentuating or reducing its raggedness, or even to imitate it.

Using a deckle From the point of view of removing sheets from the cloths, the edge produced by a tightly fitting deckle allowing no seepage underneath is the easiest edge to have, as it presents a fairly uniform edge for handling on a thin to medium-weight sheet. A slightly uneven deckle or mould may result in pulp seeping underneath, and a consequently ragged edge in that place. To remedy this, cut a piece of felt the

same size as your deckle, and glue it to the underside of the deckle using a waterproof glue. If your mould or deckle has warped a lot, you may need some force and one or two layers of felt on the deckle. Once you start to make very heavy sheets of a cardboard consistency, you will see the edges becoming more wiggly, even though the mould fits well.

Using no deckle Strictly speaking, using no deckle is technically incorrect as there will be no water retained to swish and bind the fibres together, resulting in sheets that are less strong than their cousins properly shaken on a mould with a deckle. However, the irregularity of the edges of sheets made this way adds to the handmade touch, and the tissue flimsiness of these sheets seems to impart an added preciousness and even a touch of antiquity.

▲ *Examples of the ragged deckled edge that you get to varying degrees on a piece of handmade paper.*

Set up a thin vat and simply make the sheet as usual but minus the deckle – no shaking is necessary, just bring the mould out of the water on a flat plane and keep it flat while the water runs off. Drain off excess moisture by tilting one corner back towards the vat. Press your sheet off onto a damp cloth as before. You will need to take extra care when you come to brushing the sheet off the cloth as the edge is so thin and irregular.

Imitation torn edge There is, unfortunately, no good way to recreate the effect of a very irregular edge such as that formed with no deckle. A passable edge to a well-fitting deckle is to tear the paper, but this will not bear close scrutiny. Fold the paper, crease it and then tear. Allow a few extra sheets in case this goes wrong. Take extra care when doing this with sheets which contain other ingredients (such as silk or plants); you may find that you need the help of a pair of scissors at crucial points where extra long fibres cross the edge.

COLOURING YOUR PAPER

Colour washes of paint can obviously be applied to your paper once you have made it, but it is often useful to colour the pulp before the paper is formed. Powdered or liquid tempera colours and acrylics can be used, and even tea and coffee give soft warm tones to the paper. To ensure an even distribution of colour, the pigments should be mixed with water in the liquidizer. They should then be added to the pulp and mixed thoroughly; remember to wipe any untinted pulp off the walls of the bucket and into the main body of colour.

If you are recycling a white or cream paper, you will find that dark intense colours can be difficult to achieve, as the paler colours of the base pulp tend to act in the same way as white, and brighten the overall effect. Using cold water dyes will result in darker colours. Follow the hand method described in the manufacturer's instructions. Before you beat up your pulp, you will need to know the dry weight of the paper that you intend to dye as one sachet only dyes 250g (8oz) of paper. Two tablespoons of washing soda can be substituted for the cold fix (it is much cheaper and has the same effect). After the dyeing time has elapsed, rinse the pulp well in a sieve under cold running water to get rid of the fixing agent. Then add it to the vat as required.

Once you have decided upon which colouring agent you are going to use, ensure that you mix more pulp than you will require if you are making a batch of papers, as it can be very difficult to get a perfect match on a subsequent mix. If you want to test the colour that you have mixed up before going any further, take a few fibres from the edge of the mix, and iron them dry through a tea-towel or something similar.

Pre-mixed colour can be squirted onto the sheet as soon as the mould is removed from the

▼ *Colour a sheet by squirting pre-mixed colour onto the sheet as soon as the mould is removed from the vat.*

▲ *When colour is squirted onto a newly formed sheet before couching, the colours may be further mixed as the paper is pressed.*

SIZING

Size is what newsprint lacks, so that if you write upon it with a water-based ink, the ink will be soaked up like blotting paper. Most commercial papers are sized and you will probably find, if you are using a recycled sized paper for your pulp, that your finished sheets retain sufficient size for you to be able to use a fine-tipped felt pen, roller ball or similar, without any noticeable spreading of the ink on the sheets.

However, in certain circumstances sizing is necessary, such as for watercolour painting, or for writing in ink across sheets incorporating plant pieces. Traditionally, sheets are sized with animal products and you may use these if you wish, but they can be smelly so I recommend using wallpaper paste and PVA glue. The very best results are achieved by stretching the paper first, as one would do to a watercolour, but this involves losing 2.5cm (1in) from each edge as the paper is cut free. For many purposes it is not, strictly speaking, necessary to stretch sheets before sizing them.

To stretch your paper Stretching should be done only to sheets of paper that are not less than three weeks old, as the older the sheets are the better the fibres have settled. Do not attempt to stretch poured or mould-dried sheets. Run cold water in a bowl large enough to be able to float your sheet in. Submerge the sheet in the water. Lift it out carefully, and place it on a flat clean sealed board or similar.

If your sheet has not gone down flat, lift and replace from the edges, gently pulling out ridges and creases. The larger the sheet that is to be stretched, the greater the care is needed, as the increasing weight of the water adds more strain on the binding fibres.

Cut some 5cm (2in) wide gummed brown or white tape into lengths approximately 10cm (4in) longer than the edges of your sheet for stretching. Wet the tape and stick it down along each edge of

vat (you will need another pair of hands to hold the mould and deckle while you squirt the colour). Colour can also be squirted onto the newly formed sheet before couching. This results in a more defined pattern. In both instances, as the paper is pressed the colours may be further mixed together, often to pleasing effect.

You should spare a thought for the use of the final paper. For most stationery and paper for short-lived situations, the colour that you choose will not need to be as durable as it would for paper on permanent display, such as a blind, lampshade or picture. Paint is graded in catalogues of AA, A, B and C, AA being the least fugitive colour when exposed to light, and C the most. You should therefore avoid colours in the B and C categories for items to be in constant or prolonged exposure to light.

the paper to a depth of approximately 2.5cm (1in). As the sheet dries, it will tighten like a drum skin. When the sheet is dry, apply the size of your choice, pasting it over the surface with a paintbrush. Do not cut the paper free until the size is completely dry. In this way you can only size one surface of the sheet.

▶ *To stretch a sheet of paper, first submerge it carefully in a large bowl of cold water.*

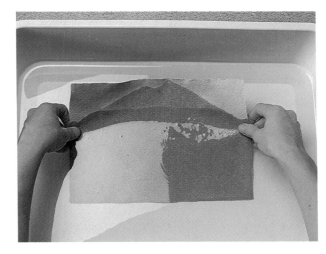

▶ *Lift the sheet out carefully and place it on a flat, clean board. Tape down the edges with wet tape and leave to dry.*

Wallpaper paste This gives an invisible coating to the paper. If you have any plants in your paper, you will notice that, after sizing, there is a slight glazing over the petals and leaves as the size has dried on them, but you need to move the paper into the light to see this glazed effect. Lay out your sheet on a clean surface. Make up approximately 625ml (1pt) of wallpaper paste by following the instructions on the packet for sizing. Brush the thick mixture onto your paper and leave it to dry. If you wish to work on both sides of the paper, you will have to size both sides. When the first side is dry, turn the paper over, paste and leave. You should not have to apply a second coat if the paste has been well spread over the paper, but you may if you wish. Having re-wetted the sheet you may need to re-press it before proceeding, but if you like the texture that you have, this is not necessary. The wallpaper paste will keep well in an airtight jar in a refrigerator, but do not use it if it is beginning to go off.

PVA glue Using a PVA size will add a slight sheen to the whole of your paper, which will be visible when you move the paper in the light. Mix 1 part PVA with 3 parts water and proceed as for wallpaper paste.

Starch Mix up the starch as for the recipe for envelope flap glue (see page 70) and apply to the sheet as for wallpaper paste.

NB: As these are all water-based techniques they will re-wet any 'unfixed' colour in your paper, for example plants which have bled colour into the paper. When the dye is re-wetted, the colour may be spread further by brushing on the size. If this is the case, you may need to spray the paper with two coats of lacquer, allowing it to dry between applications to prevent colour spreading. This, too, will add a slight sheen to the paper. If you are in a hurry to use your sheets, spraying them with lacquer is the fastest (but most expensive) option as it then dries very quickly.

TROUBLESHOOTING

PROBLEMS	SOLUTIONS
Paper too thick	Remove some of the pulp from the vat and replace it with warm water. For most things there is sufficient pulp in the vat when the mix feels like a broth-thin soup. Consider removing the deckle for making very thin sheets. Construct a lower deckle and thus retain less pulp.
Sheets of uneven thickness	Check for a badly fitting deckle allowing pulp to escape which is then forming a thinner area. In this case, either hold the mould and deckle together more firmly, or add a layer of felt with waterproof glue to the underside of the deckle. The sheet has not been properly shaken when wet. Keep practising.
Concentric rings and/or ridges on sheets	The sheet has been shaken too long in the mould. Aim to stop shaking just before the sheet stops looking fluid.
Water not draining well from the mould	The water may be too cold, so add hot water to the vat. If the hot water does not work, try adding a few drops of washing-up liquid to the vat. Check that the mould is not clogged with fibres, by washing under a running tap. There are a few plants that, when added to the vat can adversely affect the drainage as they exude a lot of thick juices. In these rare instances, you can try using a lesser concentration of the plant by adding a greater proportion of other fibres, and/or put it down to experience.
Drip marks on the sheet	These have probably been caused by water dripping onto the sheet while still on the mould, most probably when removing the deckle – so take extra care when removing the deckle, and beware of other stray splashes on the sheet when it is couched.

PROBLEMS	SOLUTIONS
Sheets too heavy to handle safely after pressing – resulting in stretch marks, or ripping where the sheets have been held	The sheets are too wet and need more pressing to expel the excess water. Try re-pressing the sheets between more absorbent layers or the second step before pressing (see page 23).
Air bubbles in couched (inverted) sheet on cloth	Viscose cloth and/or felt are too wet so that the air cannot escape. Couch onto cloths that are just damp, and use a new felt for each couching.
Unsuccessful removal of the first sheet in the pile	The first sheet is always the most difficult to couch successfully, so do not panic. Check these two points: (i) That there is enough camber on your lower board. The folded newspaper or similar should have created a slight ridge in the centre of the board. Try adding an extra layer of folded newspaper. (ii) That there is sufficient 'give' in your pile of felts, and if it seems to be a bit firm, add an extra couple of felts.
Sheet sticking to the mould	The cloths or felts that you are working with are too dry – they need to be damp. There is not enough camber on your bottom board. This can be remedied by making a slight ridge, for example by packing it with some folded newspaper. The wire/net may be too floppy to press against properly, in which case rewire/renet your mould. The wires/netting may be partially clogged with fibres, so wash them off under a running tap, at the same time giving the screen a gentle rub with a nail brush. Increasing the temperature of the vat may cure it if nothing else seems to be wrong. The pulp may have been standing on the mesh for too long. If this is the case, the fibres will sink into the mesh.

PROBLEMS	SOLUTIONS
Creases in the paper	The viscose cloth/felt had a crease in it when pressing. Take care that all of the cloths in the pile for pressing are uncreased.
Small crease at the edge of the sheet	This is a sign of hesitating while the mould was removed after pressing, thus allowing the paper at the point of hesitation to stretch slightly. Lift off the mould from one side in an unhesitating movement.
Whole sheets wrinkling or curling after drying	The sheet cannot have been 100 per cent dry before it was removed from its drying place: in all instances of drying, err on the side of caution.
Ridging of the edges of the sheet after drying	Usually a sign that the paper was not properly dry before stacking into a pile. It can sometimes be the air conditions that the paper is stored in. This causes the drying out of the edges of the sheet more than its centre, thus setting up different tensions within the sheet.
Colours from plants or other dyes, bleeding and diluting too far	The sheet has taken too long to dry – possibly press the sheets an extra time before drying and/or leave in a warmer situation to dry. If you are press drying, change the cloths more frequently, especially for the first three or so changes.
A smoother finish required	Either try another method of drying, or try filling the gaps in the paper. This may be achieved by adding china clay to the vat, known as 'loading' the paper. However, be aware that the china clay will tone down the effect of any dyes used. Start by adding to the vat a pre-mixed dry weight ratio of 1:10 china clay to your dry weight pulp. Preferably, to ensure that it is evenly distributed, mix it in a liquidizer. If this does not have the right effect, alter the ratio of china clay to pulp accordingly.

Concentric rings in sheet

Drip marks on sheet

Air bubbles in couched sheet

PURE PLANT PAPERS

The effects that can be achieved by going right back to the plant source for your fibres bring to mind materials and gauzes rather than paper. It is both satisfying and fascinating to see how the various plants turn out when processed. It also becomes apparent why papermakers within Europe preferred naturally rotted cotton and linen rags rather than plants as their sources!

Which plants to use You are looking for plants which are fibrous but not woody, for example stinging nettles, iris, bamboo leaves, straw, reeds, montbretia, nasturtium stems, etc – but you could experiment with other plants too! The plants may be used fresh or dried. The state of the original plant, and the season of the year when it was harvested will affect the final sheet. If you think that you may want to be making pure plant paper in the winter or spring it is advisable to pick and store your plants beforehand, as many of them will die down to nothing in the winter.

If picking plants to use later, you can store them by either hanging the plants upside-down in bunches and allowing them to dry, or rinsing them and placing them into plastic bags in a warm place to start rotting. Before you can use the plant fibre, it must be broken down. There are two ways of doing this, either by cooking the plants with caustic soda and water, or by leaving the plants to rot naturally.

Using caustic soda This method of breaking down plants takes about $2\frac{1}{2}$ hours. I recommend using a maximum of 250g (8oz) fresh plant material in a large stainless steel saucepan so that the pan will not be more than half full when the plant material, caustic soda and water are in place. Good fresh fibrous plant material will yield approximately 30g (1oz) of cellulose fibre.

Cut off the non-fibrous leafy parts of the plant and rinse the remaining plants to rid them of grit. Chop them into 2.5cm (1in) lengths and crush any extra thick stems.

▼ *Wearing rubber gloves, put chopped plants into a pan of caustic soda and water and press down with a wooden spoon.*

▲ *Bring the plant mixture to the boil and simmer for two hours. After this time, it will have* *reduced to a noxious black-brown gooey brew. Leave to cool.*

Wearing rubber gloves, add 2 tablespoons of caustic soda to the stainless steel pan, and 1.25 litres (2 pt) of cold water. NB: take great care when using caustic soda as it can cause burns. Follow the precautions on the tin, and wear rubber gloves when you might come into contact with traces of even diluted caustic soda. Do not use pans that are not stainless steel. Stir the water until the caustic soda has dissolved but do not inhale the fumes. Put the chopped plants into the pan, and press them down with a wooden spoon. If the plants are not covered, add up to 1.25 litres (2 pt) extra water to cover, but the pan should not be more than half full. Put the lid on and bring to the boil. Do not leave the pan unattended while it is coming to the boil, in case the caustic soda begins to spit over the top.

Reduce the heat and leave it to simmer. This is a foul process and many noxious smells are produced; I try to cook up a brew and leave all the kitchen windows open and the extractor fan on.

After two hours switch off the heat. The brew will be a black-brown gooey liquid. Leave it to cool if you wish, then strain the liquid through a plastic sieve. Rinse any remaining plant pieces into the sieve, and put the pan to one side to be washed and rinsed thoroughly.

Rinse the plants in the sieve with cold running water. When most of the black liquid has gone, squeeze and rummage through the plants to ensure that they are all properly rinsed. This will also loosen and wash away any remaining fleshy bits of plant. You need to be sure that all traces of the caustic soda have gone and allow, say, five minutes of rinsing and squeezing the plants under a slow, flowing tap.

Natural rotting If boiling up plants in caustic soda doesn't appeal, it is possible to let nature do the work for you. Pick your chosen plants and rinse them to eradicate grit, etc. Put the wet plants into a plastic bag, seal it and label it with the date and plant type. Leave the bag in a warm place until the plant material is weak enough to be broken easily by your hands.

Now, you need only wash it to get rid of any spare fleshy plant pieces before working and, if wished, you may boil the plants in ordinary water for 30 minutes to soften the fibres. Plants picked at different stages of their life will require differing rotting times, and the rotting time for each plant will also vary. I am currently using plants picked 12 months ago – but you should reckon on a minimum of 12 weeks. If the rotting is not complete, you may still have to cook with caustic soda for a lesser time. The result of all of this is a small fistful of 'hair'. You may not like the colour of the fibres you have obtained, and you may wish to make them paler or to dye them, in which case you will have to bleach them. To do this, leave the plants for the minimum time necessary in the bleach, as it will weaken the fibres.

Making the paper As you probably have relatively few fibres, you may care to consider

▼ *Rinse the plants in the sieve with cold running water for five minutes, squeezing the plants with one hand to ensure that all the caustic soda is washed away.*

▶ *Sheets made with pure plant fibre can vary in appearance from one made from 100% pure plant (top left), one made with 100% pure plant with 50% of the fibres liquidized (top right), one made with the addition of cotton pulp (bottom left), to one made with the addition of wood pulp (bottom right).*

making your smallest sheet size, especially initially, to give you a better idea of the possibilities. Very beautiful wispy sheets that are full of holes can be made by putting the unbeaten fibres into the vat and working as usual.

If you want a pure plant fibre sheet without holes you will need at least 50 per cent of the fibres to be processed in a liquidizer. Even so, these sheets are hard work to write on, but this can be improved by adding a handful or so of recycled pulp or cotton linters, or even some of your own recycled cotton/linen/silk fibres. You will have to experiment to see which effect pleases you most.

Drying Air drying of sheets with a very high percentage of plant fibres can sometimes result in badly curled, brittle sheets, which are difficult to restore to complete flatness without damaging them. Try press drying, drying on glass or drying on the mould. In the latter two cases, you will probably find a knife a great help to ease the fragile plant sheets from their drying position.

PAPERS FROM OTHER FIBRES

Cotton linters These are the next easiest to use after recycling your domestic papers. The difficulty will be to obtain them locally. Many hand-made papermakers nowadays use cotton linters as their main or only source. They come in large, thick, slightly creamy-coloured sheets that break down in a liquidizer very easily after tearing them into pieces and soaking in water until thoroughly wetted. They are comprised of fibres from the cotton plant left after the ginning operation.

You will need to add to your liquidizer less linters than the equivalent looking mass of paper for recycling as the linters fluff up a surprising amount. After you have separated the fibres by liquidizing, work as normal, and you will find that the water drains away faster than in the recycled wood pulp as the fibres in the linters are longer. The finished paper has a completely different feel to the wood pulp, being much softer. The paper made from cotton linters is also much stronger than a recycled wood paper. It is useful for projects that will be subject to a lot of wear and tear, or that you expect to last a long time.

Recycling old material Like taking the plants from your garden and converting them into paper, the satisfaction involved in writing upon what was the shirt on your back is enormous. Only materials that are 100 per cent pure cellulose may be worked with, for example 100 per cent cotton, linen or silk, the more threadbare the better as they are the strongest, longest fibres in the original garments and will make the strongest papers. The cooking time in caustic soda can apparently take up to six to eight hours! I have never cooked beyond four hours, though, as I love the effects obtained from the partially broken-down fibres.

You should follow the method used in pure plant papers (see page 36) but shred the material into smaller pieces if you have the patience. You can expect a much higher yield than with the plants. You can reduce the cooking time in caustic soda by pre-rotting your cellulose by wetting the material and putting it into a warm corner to rot, ensuring that it remains damp at all times. It is worth testing your brew after two or three hours if you have used partially rotted fibres (after four hours for unrotted fibres). To test the fibres that have been cooked in caustic soda, wearing rubber gloves, remove a few fibres on a wooden spoon, place them into a plastic sieve and wash them thoroughly. Can you pull them apart yet? If 'yes', put them into your liquidizer, whizz it up and see if they break down completely into their constituent fibres. If they do not, return them to the pan for further cooking and continue until this stage is reached.

You may decide that it is not worthwhile doing the noxious cooking, and that you are happy with the effects achieved by partially cooked or rotted fibres. After all, you can buy 'plain' well-broken down fibred paper from a good stationer.

▼ *Cotton linters come in large, thick, creamy-coloured sheets. Tear them into pieces and soak thoroughly before using them to make pulp.*

Gallery

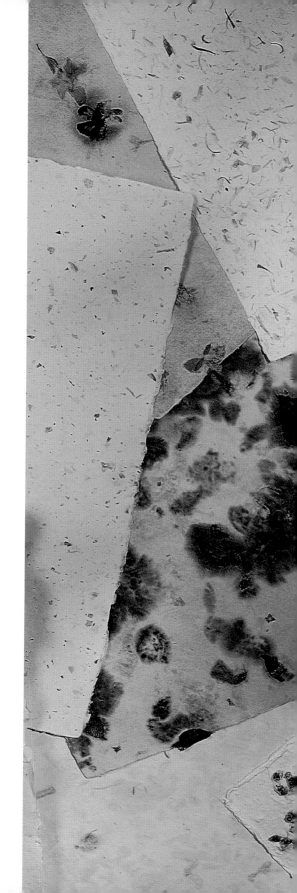

Once you have mastered the basic techniques of making paper, you can then begin experimenting with the ingredients of your paper pulp to achieve some of the more unusual and decorative papers illustrated on the following pages. Try adding flower heads, seeds, strands of silk and wool, and even more unusual ingredients such as glitter, confetti and sand – there really is no limit to what you can use to create interesting effects in your handmade paper! So, turn over the page, be inspired, and then go and discover some more startling effects for yourself!

Selection of handmade paper

THESE PAPERS HAVE BEEN CHOSEN TO GIVE AN IDEA OF the range of effects that can be achieved by adding differing ingredients to the background pulp, other than paint and dye. By increasing or reducing your ingredients, chopping them more or less finely, rotting or cooking them before addition, you will find that there is no end to the possible effects. Yet, this is only half the story; paper needs to be felt as well as seen for the full effect – the softness of a sheet made from cotton linters when compared with that of a recycled wood pulp, the smoothness of a sheet dried on glass – these textures will subtly contribute to the visual impact of the paper.

◄ *Sheets with a background of smoothly ground pulp mixed with less finely ground pulp of contrasting colours. The green sheets also contain partially ground silken scraps.*

► *Combinations of ground silken scraps with silk and woollen strands in various plain and tinted background pulps.*

◄ *The startling effects in these sheets have been achieved by adding various flower heads to a vat of bright white pulp. The sheet which is second from the back contains fresh sweet peas. The back sheet and the front two sheets contain dried pansies which were soaked in hot water for five minutes before being added to the vat. The remaining sheets contain red and yellow frozen tulips.*

▶ *Montbretia, maize husk, bamboo and stinging nettle were used fresh, boiled in plain water, cooked in caustic soda or naturally rotted and ground, to achieve the effects on these sheets. They were mixed with white pulp or laminated onto a plain white sheet to show off the fibrous nature of the plants.*

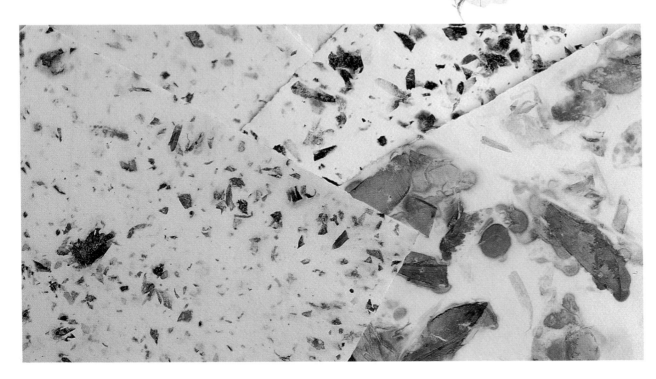

◄ *Similar pansies as were used opposite have been used here, but this time they were fresh and gave a less intense effect. When a dark red frozen tulip was mixed with pulp, it released dark green stains.*

Cornflower petals can give stunning effects. These sheets were obtained by using combinations of fresh petals, both whole and ground up, in a white ground pulp.

▶ *Cornflowers freeze wonderfully and can
then be used out of season. As they dry, the colour
in the petals bleeds into the surrounding paper – just how
much depends on how long they take to dry. Unlike the
fresh cornflowers where the reverse of the sheet is virtually
plain, the reverse of these sheets is speckled where the dye
has bled through the paper.*

▶ *An incomplete sheet of a contrasting colour has been laminated to one whole sheet. The second sheet was made fairly thin so that the different thicknesses were not apparent.*

▶ *Partially ground paper has again been added to a finely ground, tinted pulp. As with all the other papers on this page, the reverse is plainer than the top, making it an ideal writing surface.*

▶ *Confetti, lengths of gold thread, glitter and paper dots have been added to tinted vats of pulp to create these party invitation-like effects.*

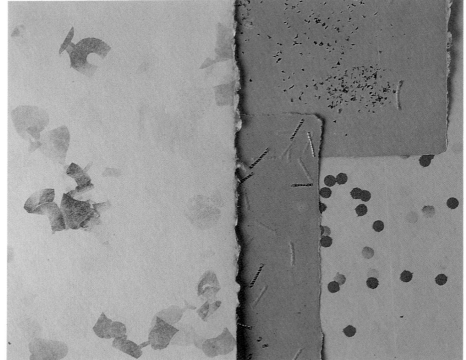

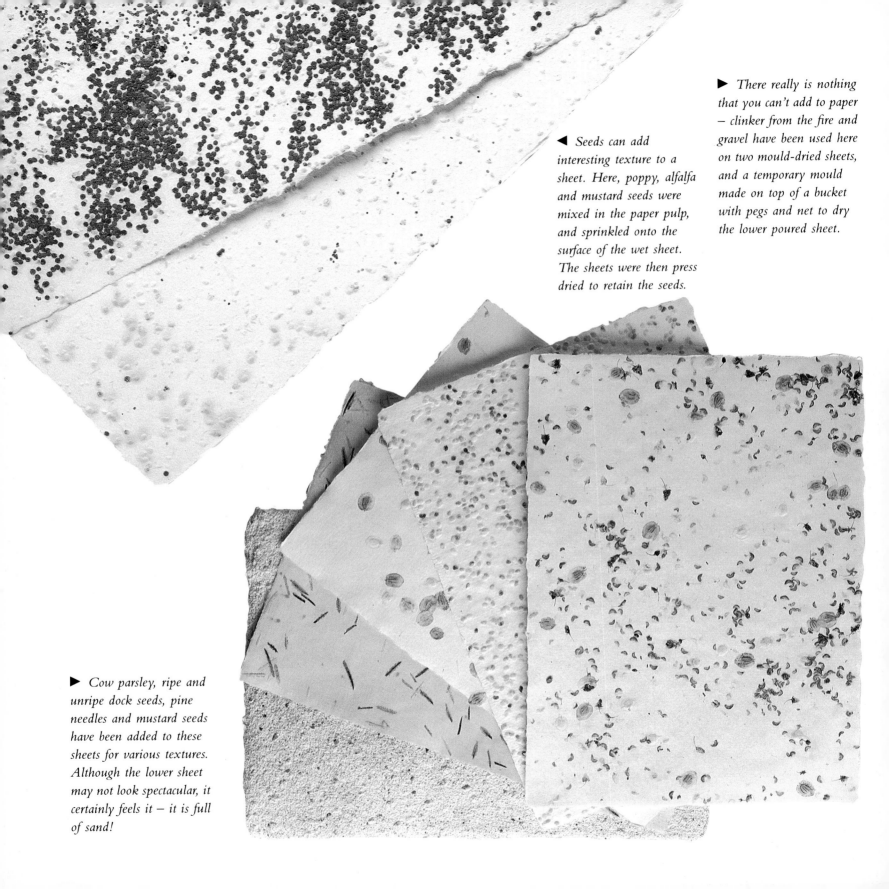

◀ Seeds can add interesting texture to a sheet. Here, poppy, alfalfa and mustard seeds were mixed in the paper pulp, and sprinkled onto the surface of the wet sheet. The sheets were then press dried to retain the seeds.

▶ There really is nothing that you can't add to paper – clinker from the fire and gravel have been used here on two mould-dried sheets, and a temporary mould made on top of a bucket with pegs and net to dry the lower poured sheet.

▶ Cow parsley, ripe and unripe dock seeds, pine needles and mustard seeds have been added to these sheets for various textures. Although the lower sheet may not look spectacular, it certainly feels it – it is full of sand!

◀ *An old cotton pillow slip and a silk shirt both cooked in caustic soda are responsible for these effects. Here you see laminations onto plain white backgrounds and mixes with plain white pulp.*

▶ *Naturally rotted and cooked maple leaves, pampas seedhead, ornamental grass, oriental poppy and the seedhead of common reed result in these more subtle effects when added to a white recycled pulp. Try using dahlia and dandelion flowers . . . the list is endless.*

Projects

These projects have been chosen to use the full range of papermaking techniques. They include quick and easy projects, such as cards, envelopes and bookmarks, as well as unusual ideas for the more ambitious including a lampshade and vertical blinds. Most are fairly inexpensive to do – all they require is your time. They are, of course, initial ideas and will hopefully lead you on to create other projects of your own.

Leaf bookmark

This is a simple project which could make an inexpensive gift, possibly with a matching card from the remaining sheet of paper. Alternatively, you could subdivide the whole of your deckle and go into bulk production of Christmas presents!

You will need:
- Ruler
- Pencil
- Saw
- Piece of wood (1 × 1cm ($\frac{1}{2}$ × $\frac{1}{2}$in)
- Vat of pulp
- Mould and deckle
- Leaves for decoration (optional)
- Felts
- Viscose cloths
- Boards
- Ribbon (optional)
- Hole punch (optional)

1 Before starting to make the paper for your bookmark, you will need to decide on the desired width and length of your bookmark, and make the appropriate divider to wedge into place within your deckle. In this way, you could if you chose, make more than one bookmark at a time. Simply cut the wood to the internal measurements of the mould where you wish to make a division. If, after cutting the wood, you find that you have cut it too short, wedge a matchstick or other sliver of wood into place. If the wood is not the same depth as the deckle, push the wooden divider down until it is flush with the underside, so that it will fit snugly against the mould surface. (If you have a net mesh on your mould, you may need to make the dividers slightly proud of the bottom to accommodate the stretch when the pulp is taken up.)

2 Unless you intend to mount your bookmarks onto card, you will probably want to make the paper fairly sturdy, so make the pulp in the vat very thick, almost like porridge. Form the sheet as usual; when the dripping has slowed and draining occurred, lift the whole deckle to reveal where no pulp has fallen.

3 At this stage you can decorate your bookmark, if you do not already have something for that purpose within the pulp. I laid a couple of leaves, vein-side down, upon the body of the bookmark before couching, and they remained in position until drying under pressure was completed. (If you would like to decorate your bookmark in this way, ensure that the leaves are completely clean on the underside before laying them against the paper.) Then they were peeled off. Any textured or patterned surface that will not damage on prolonged exposure to the damp could be substituted for the leaves. You may thread a ribbon through a punched hole at the bottom of the bookmark for a stylish finishing touch.

▲▲ *Decide on the width of your bookmark and make a wooden divider for your deckle and wedge it into the appropriate place.*

▲ *Lay clean leaves vein-side down on the body of the bookmark before couching it.*

Drawer liner

Drawer liners, delicately perfumed and decorated with pretty flowers, make lovely and thoughtful presents. If you are planning to roll up a drawer liner in order to wrap it, remember not to include plant pieces in the paper that are too large as they will come away from the paper as it is rolled.

You will need:
- Sheets of handmade paper, possibly made with pretty or fragrant flowers or seed heads, for example lavender heads
- Spray-on shoe protector
- Essential oil
- Ribbons (optional)
- Hole punch (optional)

1 Take your chosen sheet of paper and trim it to fit the drawer, if necessary. Spray shoe protector onto the side that you intend to be facing uppermost in the drawer. Allow it to dry.

2 Drip a few drops of the essential oil onto the unsprayed side of the drawer liner (lavender and lemon grass are reputed to act as insect repellants but you can use your favourite mixture), and allow it to dry.

3 The liner is now ready to go into a drawer with the oiled side facing downwards. If you need to make larger sheets to cover a drawer completely, and do not have a sheet large enough, join two or more sheets together by threading ribbons in and out through punched holes along adjoining edges. Allow at least twice the length to be joined in ribbon. To ensure the drawer liner retains the perfume of the essential oil, add a few more drops every few months or so.

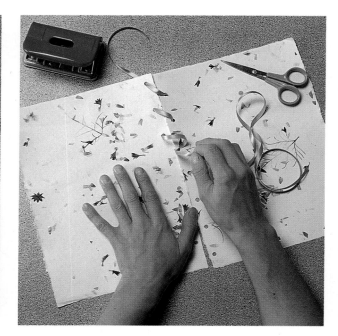

▲ *Drip a few drops of essential oil onto the side of the drawer liner that has not been sprayed with shoe protector and allow to dry. Repeat every few months to ensure the drawer liner retains the scent.*

▲ *To make a drawer liner larger than an A4 sheet, join two or more sheets together. Punch several holes along adjoining edges of the sheets, then weave ribbons in and out of the punched holes.*

Picture mount

The soft edge of these mounts offers a refreshing change from the usual straight edge of a commercially available picture mount. You can design your mount to pick up colours in the pictures that you wish to mount, or even incorporate into the paper fragments from an event or place, for example grasses and sand from your holiday around a holiday photo.

You will need:
- Cutting knife
- Plastic envelope stiffener
- Skewer
- Screw
- Vat of pulp
- Mould and deckle
- Felts
- Viscose cloths
- Boards
- Sponge

1 Select the shape and size mount that you wish to create, bearing in mind that going to within 1.5cm ($\frac{5}{8}$in) or less of the sheet edge is not advisable. Cut out the shape that you require the aperture to be from plastic envelope stiffener or thick tape-covered cardboard. Pierce the centre of your shape with a skewer, and thread the screw through the hole.

2 Set up your papermaking equipment. Place the shape that you have made into the position on the mould where you want the final aperture to be. Hold your mould and deckle firmly, with your thumbs resting on the aperture shape to prevent it floating away in the water, and make the sheet as usual.

3 After removing the deckle, dab the shape with a sponge to remove excess water, then carefully lift the shape up, holding onto the screw.

4 When couching, in addition to pressing on your deckle, you must simulate the effect of a deckle by pressing down with your finger next to the inner edge, and then remove the mould as usual. Dry and press as wished.

VARIATIONS
Multiple apertures *To make a mount with more than one aperture, you will require help to hold the shapes in place – or kitchen scale weights would do the job.*
Double mount *To give a professional finish, either make two mounts in contrasting colours in the same shape but of slightly different aperture size, or buy the mount with the smaller aperture and make the top mount to contrast. The minimum difference in size should be 1–1.5cm ($\frac{1}{2}$–$\frac{5}{8}$in) to allow for the deckle edge.*

▲▲ *Sponge off any excess water from the aperture shape, then carefully lift it up, holding it by the screw in its centre.*

▲ *When couching the sheet, press down with your finger next to the inner edge to simulate the effect of a deckle.*

Panels of paper

Notelets and especially cards are a simple way of using even your most textured, holey or creased sheets of paper. Alternatively, if you have just a little of a paper you really like, this could help eke it out. The method also avoids the conflicts of finding suitable envelopes provided that you can find a mounting card and envelope that match.

You will need:
- Handmade paper
- Scalpel
- Metal-edged ruler
- Mounting card
- Adhesive
- Powdered gold and silver tempera colours or ink
- Paper adhesive
- PVA glue
- Paintbrush
- Plant material (optional)

Cut panels
Cut your sheet of paper into panels, taking care to cut the edges parallel. Leaving one deckled edge in place can be effective. Mount the paper onto the front of the chosen card using paper adhesive.

Deckled panels
Make special panels with four deckled edges. Make up a special mould and deckle, or use a special deckle on your larger mould, or put in dividers to your ordinary deckle as in the bookmark project (see page 56).

As an inner leaf
You can purchase or even make window cards. They usually consist of three panels of similar width, folded to conceal the back of the inlaid sheet. All that you need do is to glue your chosen sheet of paper in position.

Collages
These provide the ideal opportunity to use up your disasters; tear or cut them up and reform them into 'landscapes', weavings, geometric or asymmetric designs.

Colouring the edges of your panels
Mix a heaped teaspoonful of gold or silver powdered tempera colour with a teaspoon of water, add a tiny dab of PVA, and mix well. Brush the mix onto the edge of your paper, and leave to dry before gluing to the final card.

Placing plants on the panels
To achieve an exact arrangement of plants, you can laminate two thin layers with your 'sandwich' of plants in the middle – this will result in a subtle effect. For a bolder effect lay the plants that you wish to use in position, and then carefully pour small handfuls of pulp over parts of the plant to bond it into place.

Some of the plant pieces may become detached as they air dry. Press drying will significantly increase the success rate, as will using pre-pressed flowers.

▲ *Colour the edge of a panel with gold or silver tempera colour mixed with PVA and leave to dry.*

▶ *Place leaves on a sheet and pour small handfuls of pulp over parts of the leaves to bond them to the paper.*

Randomly dyed cards

Children tend to be expert at this technique as they love squirting the paint and, in this instance, the more paint the better the results.

You will need:
- Soft plastic bottles with lids or squirting mechanisms
- Skewer
- Assortment of paint colours, one for each bottle
- Vat of pulp
- Mould and deckle
- Felts
- Viscose cloths
- Boards

1 Make two or three holes in the top of the bottles with a skewer. Push through from the outside to the inside. Do not make the holes too large, but if you find that they are so, you can partially blank them with tape. Put various paint colours in the bottles and add water so that the colours are still strong but not too thick, as they must be able to be squirted easily.

2 Make sheets as usual and either squirt in paint with the aid of another pair of hands as the sheet is removed from the vat and shaken, and/or when the sheet has drained. If you wish to keep the vat the original colour, you must squirt the paint and shake the mould away from the vat so that no colour drains through into the water. Do not skimp on the paint as you need enough to go through the viscose cloth and colour the adjacent sheets as well. Several colours can be applied simultaneously.

3 Couch the sheet as usual. Remove the sheets to a separate pile (see page 23) so that a much thinner than usual post of papers is made. Press them as hard as you can.

4 Remove the sheets from the cloths and dry. The paints will need washing out of the cloths and felts immediately to prevent them staining an adjacent sheet later. For this reason you may also care not to press dry the sheets, as you will cover so many felts with paint.

Child's hand-painted card

While making a sheet, place a child's outspread hand onto the mould. The hand should remain in place until the sheet has drained. The result is a three-dimensional shadow of the hand, best seen against the light or a darker coloured card. For an invitation, mount the sheet onto a card of contrasting colour or use a paper liner.

Greetings card messages

You can purchase sheets of standard greetings transfers to use inside or on the cover of your card. These are available in gold and silver as well as black, and they include numbers so that you can make up your own message.

▶ *Squirt paint onto a sheet as it is being removed from the vat and shaken.*

▶ *Make a sheet with a child's outspread hand in position on the mould. Keep the hand in place until the sheet has drained.*

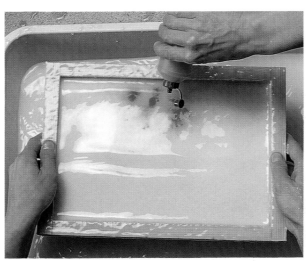

Folding invitations and cards

There are many different ways of folding a sheet of paper that may help to give a special effect for an occasion, such as a wedding invitation, an order of service, a birth announcement or a birthday party. Whichever paper you decide to create for the occasion, it is helpful to consider the colour themes or the particular floral decorations being used and to incorporate them into your paper.

You will need:
- Handmade paper
- Toning commercial paper, for lining
- Paper adhesive or needle and thread
- Sealing wax (optional)
- Ribbons (optional)
- Metal clips and fine thread (optional)

If you intend to hand-write your invitations in a water-based ink direct onto your paper, you will need to size the sheets. The paper that you create should not be so busy that the writing is obscured; though you may well find, particularly when using fresh flowers, that the top of the sheet is busy while the underside is virtually blank and, visually, presents no problems for writing upon.

If you decide to have invitations printed on your paper, you will also need to consider the 'business' of the paper. It is advisable, if you are considering this, to talk it over with a printer first and show him a similar sample of your work. Sadly, most printers do not relish the prospect of printing on handmade paper and will most

likely trim at least the leading deckled edge, that is if they are prepared to take the job on at all. To be frank, I have seldom seen the job done beautifully, so, to avoid heartache and spoiled sheets (you will need to provide extra if they go wrong), I would recommend that, if printing, you use a liner of commercial paper in a toning colour and texture.

SECURING THE LINER
Glue the printed or written liner into place with a small dab of paper adhesive. Alternatively, sew it in place using a thin needle. Before sewing, place the sheet on a board with the outside facing upwards, and then pierce the holes for the thread to go through. In this way there should be no raw edges poking through to the outside.

FASTENING A FOLDED INVITATION
All sorts of devices can be used to fasten a folded invitation. Sealing wax is available in many colours and gives an invitation a traditional feel if impressed with any hard pattern-bearing object, an initial seal, or other purchased design, over the join. Alternatively, thread ribbons through the invitation or wrap them around the outside, or punch metal clips into the paper, and then twist fine thread around them, to complete the fastening. The possibilities are endless.

JAPANESE-STYLE INVITATIONS
Take an A4 sheet, sized or not as desired. Then fold the invitation using a simple fold which allows the sheet to double up as an envelope and seal with a spot of glue.

▶ *Using this simple fold, fold a sheet so that it doubles up as an envelope. Seal with a spot of glue.*

Wallet envelopes

Before you tackle a stationery project, consider whether you want to make matching envelopes. Wallet-style envelopes are easily made from narrow sheets, but it still takes one A4 sheet to make an envelope for an A5 sheet folded in half, or an A4 sheet folded in half twice. You will need either to make yourself a template to cut your A4 sheet down, or use the same template to make up a special deckle, or fix temporary blocks into your usual A4 deckle using a water-resistant glue. The special deckle and temporary blocks will save you cutting your sheets to shape, and result in deckled edges all round.

You will need:
- Pencil
- Ruler
- Craft knife
- Plain flour
- Water
- Paper adhesive
- Envelope decorations (optional)

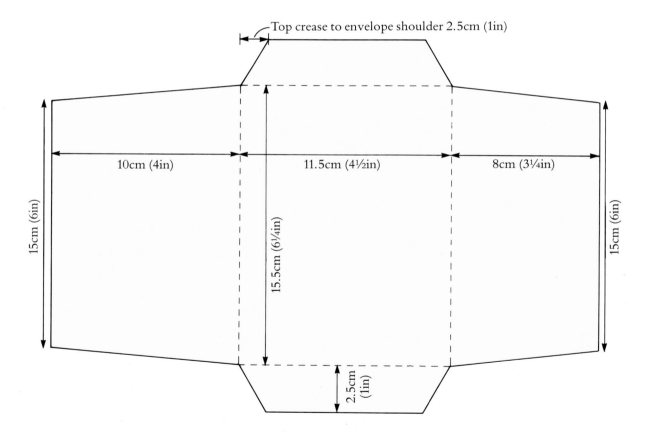

Top crease to envelope shoulder 2.5cm (1in)

10cm (4in)   11.5cm (4½in)   8cm (3¼in)

15cm (6in)

15.5cm (6¼in)

15cm (6in)

2.5cm (1in)

1 Make your template following the diagram above. This envelope has a deeper than usual top flap, to immediately differentiate your envelope from the standard commercial product, but you may wish to reduce the width and add it back onto the lower flap. Take one sheet of paper for each envelope, and cut around the template to make the basic envelope shape. In all instances, you should allow at least a 2cm (¾in) overlap to allow for glue being kept away from the contents. Score along the fold lines using a ruler and craft knife.

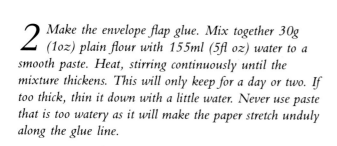

▲ Fold in the envelope flaps and apply the starch glue with a spatula.

▶ Decorate your envelope by gluing on pressed leaves, or glue a piece of paper to a corner of the envelope.

2 Make the envelope flap glue. Mix together 30g (1oz) plain flour with 155ml (5fl oz) water to a smooth paste. Heat, stirring continuously until the mixture thickens. This will only keep for a day or two. If too thick, thin it down with a little water. Never use paste that is too watery as it will make the paper stretch unduly along the glue line.

3 Fold in and glue the envelope sides. In most cases, it will be sufficient to glue the flap just before you seal it using any suitable paper adhesive, but if the envelopes are for a stationery present, you can apply starch glue to the flap with a brush or spatula. Allow the envelopes to dry with flaps open. They will stick when remoistened.

4 If you prefer, you can add further decoration to your envelope. If you have used flowers in the paper, for example, you could stick a pressed flower of the same kind to the back flap or front cover. Alternatively, you could glue a piece of paper that you have used internally to a corner or the back flap. You may need to be selective about which area of the paper you cut, opting for the 'busier' parts of the paper to give some impact. If you have tinted the edges of the piece inside, this could be done to the cut pieces before gluing into place. Another idea is to use sealing wax or small round stickers, possibly holding ribbons in place, for an olde-worlde look. If decorating a wedding invitation, for example, the wax could be used to portray the couples' initials, or some other personal motif.

Trinket box

This simple idea will make any ordinary card box and lid rather special. I have used rusty old pieces of metal and picked up the brown tints of the rust in the plain brown wrapping paper used to cover the box. But any combination of chunky or fine objects and their imprints embedded in the pulp could be used, along with a non-rusting wire or wooden handle if preferred.

You will need:
- Rusty water (optional)
- Strong small cardboard box and lid
- Paint or paper, to cover and line the box
- Iron wire
- Long-nosed pliers
- Wire wool
- Jug of pulp
- Mould and deckle
- Old nails, screws, bolts, etc (optional)
- Knife
- Spray lacquer
- Multi-purpose adhesive

PREPARATION

1 About seven to ten days before you want to make the panel, leave whatever bits of old iron that you can find in a bowl of water to make rusty water.

2 Decide which shape and size panel you wish to make for the top of your box. You may find that you can find domestic items to act as deckles, for example old plastic containers, etc. Otherwise make up your own shape from a strip of card bent and taped to the desired shape. Then either paint or cover and line your box.

MAKING THE BOX DECORATION

1 Take two or three lengths of iron wire and, using pliers, twist the wires into the desired shape for the handle, leaving long ends at each side of the handle to be embedded into the paper. Rub the handle with a pad of wire wool to scratch the surface a little, and ensure that it is properly clean.

2 Make up a jug of fairly thick pulp and add the rusty water, saving a small quantity to drip onto the surface of the panel for extra rust mottlings, if desired.

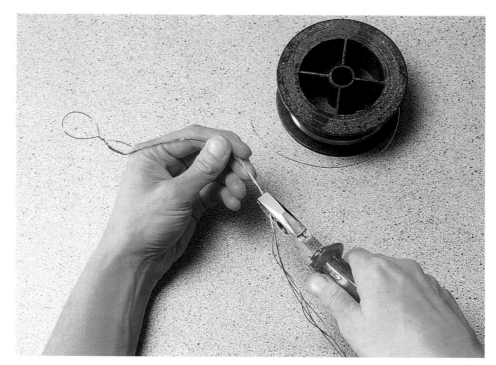

◀ *Using pliers, bend two or three lengths of iron wire into the shape of a handle, leaving long ends at each side.*

▲ *Place the wire handle in position in the pulp and pour more pulp over the handle ends to embed them into the paper.*

▶ *Push small nuts, bolts and pieces of wire into the pulp for added decoration.*

3 Place the deckle into position on the mould and, holding the mould over a large bowl to catch any drips, pour the pulp over the deckle.

4 Place the wire handle into position in the pulp in the deckle and pour a thickish mix of pulp over the handle ends to embed them into the paper.

5 Place any extra decorative nuts and bolts, wire wool, etc, on the pulp and push them into the pulp and/or pour pulp onto them. You may need to glue some into position at a later stage if they become unstuck. If you so wish, carefully drip the retained rusty water over the top where desired.

6 Leave the paper to dry. The longer it takes to dry, the greater the opportunity for the rusty marks to spread through the paper. If, when it is drying, you do not think that the effect of rust is pronounced enough, spray the paper with water to re-wet it, and leave it again. Repeat as often as necessary.

7 When you are satisfied with the extent of rust mottlings on the paper, and the sheet is completely dry, gently and carefully slide a knife under it to remove it from the mould.

8 Spray two or three coats of the spray lacquer onto the panel to seal in the rust and provide a protective outer layer. Then allow to dry.

9 Using a fast-drying multi-purpose adhesive, apply glue to the back of the panel and put it into position on the prepared box lid. Then hold it down firmly until it is dry to ensure that the panel is stuck securely.

▶ *The finished trinket boxes.*

Decorative folders

These folders have been designed with texture in mind so that the smoothness of the inner sheets contrasts with the texture of the folder. They make ideal containers for your stationery and are a great presentation for silk scarves.

You will need:
- Vat of pulp
- Mould and deckle
- Felts
- Piece of polycotton large enough to overlap the board edges
- Damp cloth
- Piece of wood thin enough for a peg to grip the edge and large enough to support your sheet
- Pegs
- Metal ruler
- Scissors
- Scalpel
- Card
- Brush
- PVA glue
- Wool/silk threads

PREPARATION

First, plan your intended folder. To construct one that will hold A4 sheets flat, you need to laminate four A4 sheets together as shown (below, top). A5 sheets need two A4 sheets to be laminated along one edge (below, bottom). I made the two folders as illustrated below, but the variations on this theme are endless.

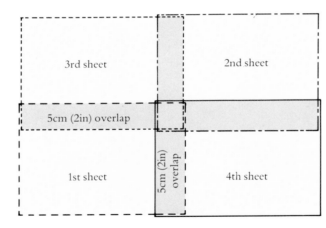

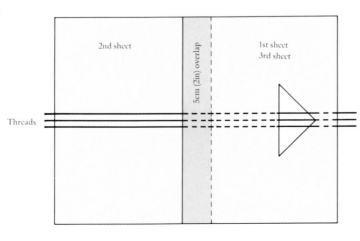

PLAIN GUSSET FOLDER FOR A4 SHEETS

1 Set up the vat with a fairly thick pulp mixture. Instead of setting up felts into a pile on a board, spread the damp felts out, hinge-butting them to cover an area slightly larger than the finished sheet. Lay down four layers of felt with the joins at different places. Smooth the piece of damp polycotton onto the top.

2 Make the sheets and couch them directly onto the polycotton, overlapping the edges. Do not worry about air bubbles. Taking a damp cloth or sponge, press the air bubbles out, forcing them to travel to the edges. Then scrunch up the cloth and press it firmly onto the whole sheet, squeezing out the cloth as it fills with water, and continue until the desired texture is achieved.

▲ *Using a scrunched-up cloth, press down firmly over the sheet to create a bumpy, textured effect, squeezing out the cloth as it fills with water.*

3 Lift the polycotton sheet and paper, paper-side up, onto a board and spread it out carefully. (If you are using an unsealed wooden board it may be worth covering it with a plastic bag or clingfilm to prevent the wood staining the paper, as the sheet takes several days to dry.) Peg down the edges of the polycotton to the board approximately 5–7.5cm (2–3in) apart and leave to dry. When dry, peel the paper from the polycotton.

4 Fold the paper, ensuring that the creases are parallel by folding around an envelope or similar of the correct width, and avoid including the laminated seams in the fold. You need a lower flap of approximately 10cm (4in), a back of 24cm (9½in) and the remainder for the top flap. Trim the outer edges parallel at the required width approximately 32cm (12¾ in) wide, and, using a scalpel, cut out the pattern on the leading flap.

5 Construct a gusset to hold the lower lip in place. Matching card is preferable but not essential. Cut two pieces of card to just under the height of the lower lip of the wallet and approximately 10cm (4in) long. Fold the paper in half (if using a textured paper, first fold the texture to the outside) and, leaving 12mm (½in), reverse the fold on both halves of the sheet to form a W. Glue into position at the edges and weight it down while it dries.

DECORATED FOLDER FOR A5 SHEETS

1 Repeat step 1 as above. Lay a cardboard triangle on the mould while the first sheet is made and couch it. Couch the second plain sheet and lay the woollen lengths into position as shown. Make a third with the cardboard triangle in the same position as the first. Laminate the third sheet into position on top of the first, aligning the triangles as closely as possible.

2 Press and dry the sheets as above. Fold the paper once just above the triangle side of the overlap to give a front flap of approximately 15cm (6in), and trim the outer edges parallel to give a total width of 26.5cm (10½in). Cut the back flap to a length of 19cm (7½in). From another card cut the shown shape to fit 6mm (¼in) from the top of the fold of the back flap. Then glue the newly constructed card shape with PVA glue and weight it down while it dries.

◄ Lay the polycotton sheet and paper onto a board and spread it out carefully. Peg down the edges and leave to dry for several days.

◄ Fold the sheet into the shape of a folder and cut out a pattern on the leading flap. Glue a gusset into each side edge.

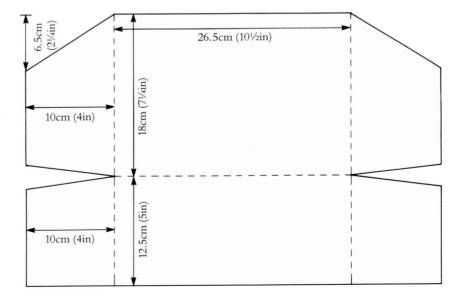

6.5cm (2¼in)

26.5cm (10½in)

10cm (4in)

18cm (7¼in)

10cm (4in)

12.5cm (5in)

Cheque book cover

Follow the given dimensions to make a cover for a cheque book measuring 19.5 × 7.5cm ($7\frac{3}{4}$ × 3in). For other sizes, you will have to amend the sizes of board, paper and ribbon, but keep the gaps and overlaps as given in the diagram.

You will need:
- Handmade A4 sheet or two A5 sheets
- Spray-on shoe protector
- PVA glue
- Stiff card/mounting board
- Scalpel
- Metal-edged ruler
- Length of ribbon, 6mm ($\frac{1}{4}$in) wide
- Lightweight card in contrasting colour, for lining
- Iron-on material, such as buckram or other woven cloth, for the spine

1 Coat your handmade paper with a layer of spray-on shoe protector.

2 Using a scalpel and a metal-edged ruler, cut out two pieces of board measuring 20 × 8cm (8 × $3\frac{1}{4}$in), being careful to cut them square. Cut out a third piece of board measuring 12mm × 8cm ($\frac{1}{2}$ × $3\frac{1}{4}$in).

3 Cut out your iron-on material to measure 9 × 12cm ($3\frac{1}{2}$ × $4\frac{3}{4}$in). If the material lets PVA through, it will have to be sealed with a coating of shoe protector on the outside. Spray on a coat of shoe protector, leave to dry, then continue. Place the material face-down onto the work surface, and, using a brush or spatula, coat it with PVA glue on the 'wrong' side. Lay out the three boards side by side in the centre of the material, as shown right, leaving a 3mm ($\frac{1}{8}$in) gap between the boards.

4 Fold the material over the spine at the top and bottom, and press down firmly.

▲ *Lay out the three boards on the iron-on material, leaving a gap between each. Fold the material over at the top and bottom.*

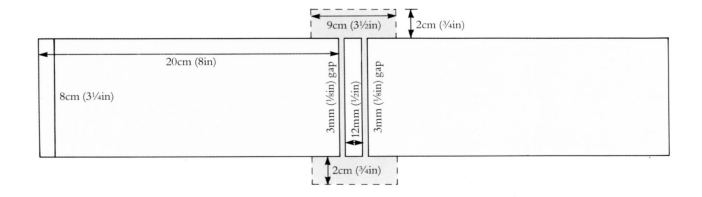

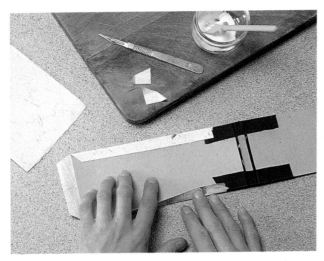

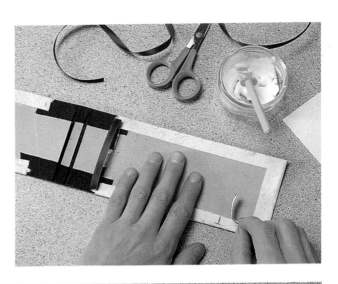

◀ *Glue the front cover in place, overlapping the spine, and fold the corners in. Wipe off excess glue. Repeat for the back cover.*

▶ *Glue the ribbons in position on the inside back cover. They should be slack enough to allow the end pages of a cheque book to pass through.*

5 *Using a scalpel and metal-edged ruler, cut two pieces from your paper to measure 19 × 11.5cm (7½ × 4½in). Place one sheet right-side down onto the work surface and put one cover into position with a 3mm (⅛in) overlap onto the spine material. Cut out 120° at the corners and fold the edges over. Remove the cover.*

6 *Cover the inside of the fitted piece with a coating of PVA glue, and place it onto a clean work surface. Put the cover into place, press it down firmly and fold the corners in. Wipe off any excess glue. Repeat for the other side of the cover.*

7 *Cut two strips of ribbon 10.5cm (4¼in) long. Stick down approximately 12mm (½in) of the ribbons to the inside back cover, 3mm (⅛in) from the top and bottom edges at 2.5cm (1in) and 15cm (6in) from the central board edge. The ribbons should be slack enough to allow a few end pages of the cheque book to pass through. Put it under weights and leave to dry.*

8 *Cut a piece of contrasting lightweight card to line the cheque book, measuring 7.5 × 40.5cm (3 × 16¼in). (There should be 3mm (⅛in) of the cover paper showing on all edges. Adjust if necessary.)*

9 *Cover approximately 20cm (8in) of the reverse of the lining card with PVA glue then slide the card through the ribbons, the unglued end first. Press own firmly when in position.*

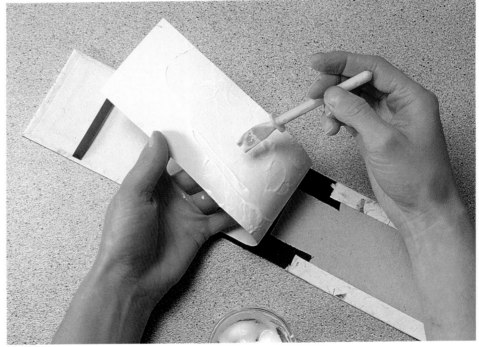

10 *Apply PVA glue to the remaining lining card and press into position. Leave to dry in the open position under pressure.*

VARIATION

You could cut off the deckled edge on the side against the spine, or tip the corners of the cheque book cover with cloth.

▲ *After attaching the ribbons, slide the lining card through the ribbon and glue in place.*

▶ *The finished cheque book cover.*

Notebook

In this project all the papers in the book are handmade. You could of course reduce the number of sheets used by substituting suitable commercial papers, or by reducing the number of pages in the book. You can also use the same technique to make a larger book.

You will need:
- 14 pieces of A5 matching paper
- Wooden board
- Scalpel
- Metal-edged ruler
- Needle
- Cotton thread
- Candle
- Scissors
- Bias binding facing material
- Two A5 neutral or contrasting sheets, for the end papers
- PVA glue
- Stiff card/mounting board
- Iron-on material, eg buckram, for the spine
- Brush
- Pen

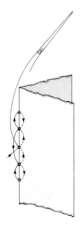

THE INSIDE OF THE BOOK

1 Take 12 of the matching A5 sheets and divide them into three groups of four. Face all of the sheets right-side up, and fold them in half widthways.

2 Place one of the sets of four sheets right-side up on the wooden board. Pierce five small holes through the layers with a scalpel, along the centre fold at 2.5, 5, 7.5, 10 and 12.5cm (1, 2, 3, 4 and 5in) from one of the outer edges. Repeat this for the two other groups, always using the same side to measure the hole spacing.

3 Thread a needle with double cotton that has been run along a wax candle a few times (this lends extra strength to the cotton). Taking one of the pierced sets, sew into the central hole from the side that will become the spine. Weave the needle and thread in and out as shown, so that the last cotton comes out of the same hole as the first. Avoid putting the needle through the ready-threaded cotton, to prevent it from tangling. Tie a double knot around the long central thread. Cut off ties at 12mm ($\frac{1}{2}$in) lengths. Repeat for the remaining two sections except for the last section, when you should proceed as before, but do not cut off the cotton thread.

4 Use the remaining cotton to thread a weave in between the cotton ties, weaving the length of the spine and back. When complete, tie off with a double knot and cut off the thread with 12mm ($\frac{1}{2}$in) ties remaining.

5 Cut a 14cm (5$\frac{1}{2}$in) length of the self-adhesive interfacing material, and iron it on around the spine as tightly as possible. Alternatively, you could use three or four material tapes, 12mm ($\frac{1}{2}$in) wide, glued around the spine to extend 2cm ($\frac{3}{4}$in) on the pages of the book.

▲▲ *Using a scalpel, pierce five small holes through the layers of the sheets at 2.5cm (1in) intervals.*

▲ *Using a needle and double cotton, sew the layers together, weaving the needle in and out of the holes.*

6 Fold the two plain sheets in half widthways. Place a piece of waste paper inside the first page to extend over the edges. Paste PVA glue onto the outside of the first page, right up to the edges and, lining it up carefully, stick on one of the plain sheets. Repeat for the back page and the last remaining sheet. Remove the protective sheets from the inside after removing any excess glue, and place them under a weight to dry.

THE COVER

1 Protect the cover sheets by spraying on a coat of shoe protector and leaving it to dry.

2 Cut the two boards to about 15.5 × 11.5cm (6$\frac{1}{4}$ × 4$\frac{1}{2}$in). This measurement depends on how ragged your deckled edges are; the boards should overlap the edges by 3mm ($\frac{1}{8}$in) on three opening sides.

3 Remove the inside of the book from its weighted position and press between the newly cut boards to check that they fit. If correct, measure the width from one outer edge to the other. Cut a spine for the book as long as the boards and as wide as the total measured width.

4 Cut the material for the spine to approximately 9 × 19cm (3$\frac{1}{2}$ × 7$\frac{1}{2}$in). (You need an overlap of approximately 2–2.5cm ($\frac{3}{4}$–1in) at the top and bottom of the book.) Test a small patch of the material to find if the PVA glue goes through to the front side. If it does, spray with shoe protector and move it to another position to dry. When it is dry, mark the centre line with a pen. Brush on the PVA glue. Place the centre of the 'spine' board along the central line, allow a 3mm ($\frac{1}{8}$in) gap and place on the cover boards to the right and the left. Check the measurements before pressing them down firmly. All three of the boards must be in alignment at the top and bottom. Fold over the excess material into the inside at both ends.

5 Take one of the two remaining pieces of paper and place them face-down. Position one board in the required position over the paper, overlapping the paper onto the spine to the preferred width. Fold over the upper and lower edges. Trim the remaining edge to a width of 2.5cm (1in). Cut across at the corners at 45°, 2.5cm ($\frac{1}{2}$in) from the corner and fold.

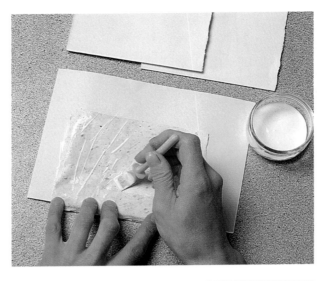

◀ Paste PVA glue onto the outside of the first page, right up to the edges, and stick it on one of the plain sheets.

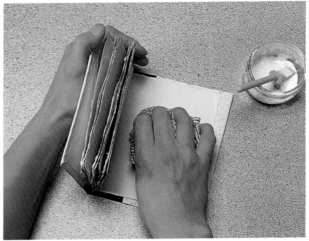

◀ Insert the centre sections of the notebook, applying extra PVA glue as necessary and pressing with a cloth to smooth out any air bubbles.

6 Cover the inside of the paper up to the edges with PVA glue. Place the sheet on a clean surface and put the book back into position. Fold the upper and lower edges and then the outer edge, applying extra PVA as necessary to the doubled folds. Smooth out any air bubbles and press firmly. Repeat for the other cover paper.

7 Place a protective sheet under the fly leaf page at one end and cover the outside page to its edges with PVA glue. Remove the protective sheet and stick it into position carefully on the front inner board, working from the spine outwards. Repeat for the back cover, and brush PVA onto the spine before stitching the cover down. Remove any excess glue then leave it under a weighted board to dry.

*P*lace mat

Paper is a very good insulating material, and is therefore ideal for making table mats. This project uses the technique of laminating, so that you have two layers of paper sandwiching a layer of pansies in between.

To achieve a good protective layer, you will have to set up your vat with so much pulp that it feels like porridge. To do the laminating thinly enough, so that you can see the encaptured pansies, you will need a second vat, set up with very little pulp. Alternatively, you could make the thick sheets and spread them out on their cloths, readjust your vat and then add the second sheet to the first, on the top of a fresh felt. To prevent the flowers from 'melting' too quickly, and becoming difficult to handle, make these sheets in a cool air temperature and a cool vat.

1 Pick blue and/or black pansies when they are dry. (Blue pansies are best, and look good combined with some black ones. If you have to pick them when it is wet, be sure that they are dry before putting them into the freezer.) Spread the flowers and stems onto a baking tray or similar. Do not overlap the plants. Put them into the freezer. Ensure that the plants are completely frozen before working with them, or the effect will not be so good.

2 Make a thick sheet using a deckle to retain the maximum possible amount of pulp. Couch it onto a cloth as usual.

3 Take the tray of pansies from the freezer. Pick up each pansy with a pair of tweezers and position it on your sheet. Continue until you have an arrangement that pleases you – bear in mind that what you see will diffuse somewhat as it dries. Return the pansies to the freezer as soon as you have taken what you need. If you have to rearrange the pansies, use the tweezers – the heat from your hand could melt the petals.

4 When you have an arrangement that you like, make a second very thin sheet without the deckle. Make a few small holes in the sheet while still on the mould where the pansies will be, so that a part of the petal will be exposed, and the veining will be visible in the finished sheet. Ensure that the pansies have 'melted' before pressing the second sheet into position. If the pansies still seem to be frozen, breathe on them for a few seconds.

5 Repeat the procedure for each mat, putting two felts between each sheet to ensure that no dye from one sheet will inadvertently stain another. When finished, put the board on top of the final felt, and press.

▲ *Using tweezers to handle the frozen pansies, to avoid melting the petals,* *arrange them individually on the sheet until you have a design you like.*

6 Use the 'press dry' method for drying, using two dry felts between each sheet in its cloth. Every time you change the felts, peel back the viscose cloth on the top side and have a look at the paper. The dye will keep spreading. When you have an effect that you like, increase the frequency of felt changing to, say, once an hour, so that the effect will not spread any further. When the sheet is 100 per cent dry, remove it from the cloth. You will have to wash both the felts and the cloths that have been stained in a mild bleach solution to remove the dye that will reactivate when it is wet, as it may otherwise stain any later sheets that it comes into contact with.

7 To protect your finished mats, using rubber gloves and a cotton wool ball, rub cellulose dope into the surface. Give one good coat to each side, allowing them to dry before turning them to the second side. Take great care when doing the deckled edges. Then press under a large book, if necessary, when dry. If cellulose dope is not available, polyurethane gloss or matt varnish may be painted on, but it does not give the virtually invisible finish of the cellulose dope.

8 Alternatively, cut a piece of hardboard approximately 5cm (2in) larger in each direction than your sheet. Paint the sides and the edges that will be exposed with size, undercoat and gloss paint of your chosen coordinated colour, allowing each coat to dry before applying the next. Apply cellulose dope or polyurethane varnish to the front of the paper as above. When dry, fix into place, using a non-water-based glue and being very careful to ensure that the deckled edges are firmly stuck. If you have used polyurethane varnish, you can give a final coat to the top of the finished mat to help the deckled edges to stick. Cover the back of the board with felt and glue in position. Alternatively, you can take your chosen sheets to a printer for lamination between two layers of plastic for an effect similar to an ID card.

VARIATIONS

Different flowers may be used; experiment, but as a rule of thumb, you will find that the darker the petals, the more intense is the colour that is yielded. Different-coloured pulps can be used, but they will tint each other, for example reds will change whites to pinks. If you are using two colours, place the darker colour down first, even if this means placing the flowers on backwards.

To make matching napkin rings, use a combination of the bookmark method (see page 56) and this place mat method. Punch or pierce the long 'bookmark' into a loop fastened with an appropriate thread or ribbon, and coat it in a layer of cellulose dope.

▶ *The finished place mats.*

◀◀ *As the paper dries, the dye will spread. Peel back the viscose cloth on the top side to check the effect on the paper.*

◀ *To protect your finished mat, rub a coat of cellulose dope into the surface using a cotton wool ball and wearing rubber gloves.*

Pendant lampshade

An attractive shade can be made with four A4 sheets. Thin sheets are preferable to thick sheets, as they allow more light to pass through them. The sheets can be plain, coloured or patterned as you choose to suit your decor – these contain lengths of embroidery silks. There is no reason why poured sheets should not be used, though these are slightly more fragile and it would be worth adding wallpaper paste to the pulp for extra strength.

You will need:
- 4 sheets of A4 handmade paper
- Craft knife
- Ruler
- Board to cut on
- Brush
- Vegetable cooking oil
- Saw
- Wooden moulding, in proportion to sheet and with at least one flat edge, 16 times the sheet width plus 1.2m (48in)
- Masking tape
- Sandpaper
- Pen
- Drill
- PVA glue
- Round wooden dowel, approximately 30cm (12in) long
- Wire, 2mm ($\frac{1}{8}$in) wide, or a metal coat hanger
- Wire cutters
- Wood stain (optional)
- Cocktail sticks
- Spray-on fire-retardant

Careful measuring, cutting and drilling are essential for this project for the lamp to hang correctly.

1 Trim the paper to exactly the same length, ensuring that the trimmed edges are parallel with the deckled side edges. (If you trim these edges also, you will need to reduce the moulding lengths accordingly.) Brush cooking oil onto one surface and leave the oil to be absorbed for a couple of hours. When the sheets are completely translucent, wipe off any excess oil and leave them overnight to dry completely.

2 Using a saw, cut the moulding into 16 equal lengths, 7.5cm (3in) wider than your paper width. Sand off any uneven pieces at the ends to leave a smooth finish. Stain and leave to dry if required.

3 Mark the centre point on the inside face of eight of the lengths of wooden moulding. Then mark the centre point at the top and bottom edge of each of the four handmade sheets.

◀ *Position a sheet onto a piece of glued moulding, aligning the centre points. Then place a second piece of moulding on top, sandwiching the paper in between.*

4 *Apply PVA glue to one marked and one unmarked piece of wooden moulding. Press down a sheet onto one piece of moulding at 1mm ($\frac{1}{16}$ in) from the top edge, aligning the marked centre points. Place the second piece of moulding onto the first, sandwiching the paper in between. Ensure that the moulding ends are level, then press and tape the ends together. Repeat for both ends of all sheets. Weight and leave to dry.*

5 *Remove the tape. Decide which edges are to be at the top of the lampshade. Mark the centre point on the inside face of each top edge of the wooden moulding. Drill three-quarters of the way through the total depth at the marked point.*

6 *Drill through all of the ends of the wooden moulding at 3mm ($\frac{1}{8}$ in) away from the paper in the same direction as the paper lies within the wood. (It is easiest to drill the moulding from the side without the paper.)*

7 *Cut a length of wire or coat hanger and form the wire into a circular loop by winding it around the light fitting (disconnect the light fitting first). Leave ends long enough to reach the drilled holes. Repeat to give a second loop, but this time allow extra length to the ends so that they can be bent down further to the lower level mouldings. Link the two loops together and bend the long lengths of the second loop down. Cut the wire ends so that they will reach three-quarters of the way through the drilled mouldings.*

8 *Lay out the lamp ready for gluing the corners by overlapping the lower lamp edge as shown. Take a cocktail or other wooden stick to fit the drilled holes and cover enough of the stick to fit through two holes with PVA glue. Put the glued stick through the two aligned holes, cut off any excess and wipe off excess glue. Repeat for all joints. You may need a second pair of hands when you come to the top edge.*

9 *Check the lengths of the wire lamp fitting and adjust if necessary. Glue the ends of the wires and insert into position in the drilled holes, with the longer pieces of wire going to the lower holes of the lampshade. Spray the lampshade with fire-retardant for safety.*

10 *Hang the lampshade. Stain any unstained exposed ends of wood if necessary. If the shade is not hanging quite square after 24 hours, you could stick small pieces of plasticine to the inside of the wooden mouldings to adjust the balance. To maintain your lampshade, vacuum it occasionally to avoid a build-up of dust, and wipe it with a damp cloth as necessary.*

▲ *Drill three-quarters of the way through the inside face of each top edge of the wooden moulding.*

◀ *To assemble the lamp, overlap the corners. Glue the moulding lengths together with small wooden cocktail sticks.*

▶ *Make circular wire loops for the light fitting, leaving ends that are long enough to reach the drilled holes in the wooden moulding.*

◀ *Check the lengths of the wire fitting and adjust if necessary. Glue the ends of the wires in the drilled holes in the moulding.*

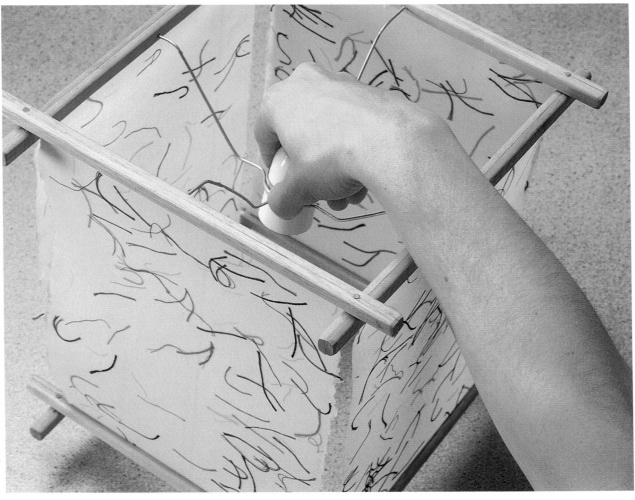

Vertical blinds

Even if you have a window larger than you can sensibly construct one single piece of paper, you will still be able to make these blinds – be it by making several pieces of paper of the correct length or even many smaller pieces glued together to make a mosaic.

You will need:
- Wooden frame to act as a mould
- Fine unpatterned nylon net to cover the mould
- Drawing pins
- Bucket of pulp – approximately 22g ($\frac{3}{4}$oz) dry weight per sq 30cm (12in)
- Bricks
- Jug
- Spray-on shoe protector
- PVA glue
- Knife
- Pegs
- Wooden moulding, 3 or 4 times the total blind width
- Saw
- Sandpaper
- Wood stain (optional)
- Fine wire
- Craft knife
- Long straight edge
- Pencil
- Right angle
- Blind mechanism
- Screw-in eye cups and chain (optional)
- Cord or chain (optional)

ORDERING THE BLIND MECHANISM

The mechanism for these blinds is made to order to your specific requirements, so before ordering you will need to know:

- The measurements of the window recess in which the blind is to hang, or, if fixing the blind outside the recess, its 'in the room' width. For an 'in the room' hanging, I add an extra 20cm (8in) to the width of the window to ensure a good overlap at the edges to exclude the light.

- Whether you want the blinds to be able to glide to both edges (as a conventional curtain), or if a one-way glide is required.

- If you are going to have 9cm ($3\frac{1}{2}$in) or 12.5cm (5in) vanes (the hanging strips). As the paper tends to be lighter than material, a 12.5cm (5in) vane is preferable in most cases as it is heavier.

  When ordering, tell the seller that you need the mechanism only, not weights or bottom chains, because, if you decide to use them, you will need to use another system than that described. When collecting your mechanism, ensure that you have the correct fixing, that is for wall or ceiling mounting.

BEFORE YOU BEGIN

Before constructing your sheet you will need to consider several things:

- Do you want the edges to be trimmed straight or do you wish to show off the deckled edge? If incorporating the deckle, will it be at the lower edge or at the sides only? If the latter, you will need to be able either to construct the sheet in one piece or to make two pieces to match, and to discard the two central edges.

- How (if at all) do you intend to colour or decorate your pulp? If using pigments, the light-fast nature has to be considered. If using plants or material additions, test them first on a small piece to establish if the colours are waterproof and, if not, that they react in the way in which you intend on prolonged exposure to water, as the paper may well take a few days to dry.

- Do you intend to pour your sheet in a random or specific pattern (how you pour will be visible when the sheet is dry), or 'paint' it into a picture using differently coloured pulps? If you intend to 'paint' it, bear in mind that it is usually best to work in a bold fashion, as controlling small amounts of pulp is difficult.

CONSTRUCTING THE WOODEN MOULD

Make a simple wooden mould using 5 × 2.5cm (2 × 1in) timber; screw and glue the pieces together as in the mould construction (see page 13). You do not need a deckle. Ideally, the mould should be as wide as the blind needs to be, and a few centimetres longer. If it is not possible to make a sheet as large as the blind requires, before you make the mould calculate how you are going to fit the sheets together, allowing distances for trimming. As usual, ensure when stringing the mould that the net is as taut as it can be.

MAKING THE SHEET

1 Make the pulp. If using a combination of different colours, split the mix into different buckets and dye sufficient in one go. (It may be helpful to have a sketch of how you intend to pour the pulp so that you can calculate the proportion of each colour required.) I usually mix each 30g (1oz) of dry weight paper into approximately 940ml (30fl oz) total volume of water, but bear in mind that each pulp pours differently. Be prepared to dilute or remove water if you find that you do not like the effect as you pour; you can scrape the pulp off and start again with adjusted pulp. You can, if you wish, also adjust the proportion of water as you go along to give a different effect, but bear in mind that depending on which (if any) colouring agent you are using, you may also dilute the colour in your final sheet.

2 Set up your mould on a few bricks to raise it from the floor, the higher the better to avoid the floor-bound dust. The mould needs to be in a place where the floor can get very wet as the mould stays in position at least overnight. Using a jug, pour your sheet. Aim to cover the net completely, even if only thinly, as areas that are uncovered are more prone to tear when removing from the mould. Leave the sheet to finish dripping (at least overnight), and re-check for any areas of visible net; if there are any, pour on more pulp and again leave it until it stops dripping.

3 To speed the drying process, remove the mould from the wet area if possible (or if applicable, remove the water on the floor), and lean the mould on end (see page 29) to dry thoroughly. Do not put it in this position until you are sure that it will not slip down the net.

4 When dry, leave the mould on end and spray with shoe protector. Allow it to dry thoroughly.

5 Carefully remove the sheet from the net, using a blunt knife and by sliding your hand behind the sheet as you push the net away from the paper.

6 Place the sheet face-down on the net and use pegs to attach the sheet to what will become the top edge of the blind. Stand the mould on end and coat with spray-on shoe protector. If you cannot make your blind immediately, it is best if you can store the sheet flat. If you must roll it, do so only loosely as this thick paper is prone to cracking and fracture when bent.

CONSTRUCTING THE BLIND

1 Select a moulding that will be in proportion to your window; it must have at least one flat surface to glue the paper to. If required, stain your moulding the day before. Cut the moulding to the selected vane width. You will need two cut lengths of moulding for each vane top, and one for each lower edge if you intend to leave the deckled edge, or two for each lower edge if you intend to

▶ *Carefully remove the sheet from the net using a blunt knife and by sliding your hand behind the sheet for support.*

▶▶ *Place the sheet face-down on the net and attach with pegs. Then coat the paper with spray-on shoe protector to seal.*

have a trimmed edge to reflect the top edge. Sand the rough edges and, if necessary, stain the ends.

2 Cut the fine wire into 20cm (8in) lengths and double each length. Then twist each wire into a loop to fit onto the hook on the blind mechanism and splay the spare lengths out sideways. (I used the handle of a wooden spoon to ensure that all loops were the same size.) Make one loop for each vane.

3 Cut the paper to the required length by cutting the top edge straight and, if no deckled edge is required, the lower edge also, ensuring both edges are parallel. Before cutting the paper into selected vane widths, calculate your cuts and mark with a light pencil on the reverse. It is usually best to have two slightly thinner outer edges rather than one regular width and one very thin vane as the thin vane will lack both self-weight and moulding weight, and it will tend not to hang true. Use a right angle to ensure that the edges are parallel and at 90° from the top edge or the vanes will not hang properly.

4 Take two lengths of cut moulding and check that they fit the paper width. (If not, either trim the paper or wood to fit.) Mark the centre width on one of them. Paste PVA glue onto the marked face and one face of the remaining piece. Place the wire loop onto the marked centre point with the loop protruding over the top sufficiently to hang the vane onto the blind's hook. Put the vane face-up on top and glue the second piece of moulding face-down onto the paper vane. Weight it firmly to dry. Repeat for all vanes, ensuring that the wire loop protrudes the same distance from each.

5 If the lower deckled edge is retained for the vanes, check that the moulding width fits the paper. Apply PVA glue onto one side of the moulding and place the moulding on the reverse of the blind at the lowest common point to all sheets at which the paper is still the regular width. Weight it and leave to dry. Repeat for all of the vanes, reducing moulding lengths for outer vanes as before if necessary. Hang them when dry. If no lower deckled edge is retained, stick the moulding lengths front and back, ensuring they are all the same length. Weight them to dry and then hang the blind.

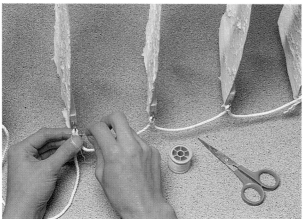

▲ Place a wire loop onto the marked centre point of the PVA-coated cut moulding so that the loop protrudes over the top. Cover with a vane and the second cut moulding.

◀ Thread cord or chain through the lower loops of the blind and sew into place at each loop.

6 If 'chains' are required, when dry, screw one hook into the centre of the side of each of the back mouldings. Hang the blind and spread out the vanes into the extended position so that each vane faces 'side-on'. Thread your chosen cord or chain through the loops on the side facing you, and sew into place at each loop once you are sure that it is in the correct position and that the vane is vertical. Tie off at the outer vanes. If you have used cord, sew the ends to prevent them unravelling. Repeat for the second side. To maintain your blinds, vacuum them occasionally to avoid a build-up of dust, and wipe with a damp cloth as necessary.

Glossary

Cotton linters Pre-beaten fibres which come originally from the cotton plant. They are obtained after the ginning process is complete. The fibres are formed into large sheets ready for pulping.

Couching The process of removing the newly-made sheet from the mould onto the post.

Deckle The removable wooden frame that sits on the mould to define the paper edge.

Felt A woollen 'sheet' of the appropriate size onto which the newly-made sheets were traditionally couched. (In this book the single felt is replaced by an old blanket or similar and a protective fine-weave viscose, cotton or polycotton cloth.)

Mould The wooden frame and wire/net that the sheet of paper is made on. There are traditionally two types of mould – 'laid' and 'wove'. The 'laid' gives rise to 'laid sheets' which reveal the ladder-like pattern of the mould wire, and a 'wove mould' gives rise to 'wove sheets' in which no discernable pattern is usually visible.

Post The pile of newly-made alternating couched papers and felts formed on a cambered board.

Pulp A mix of fibre and water.

Size A substance added to paper that prevents it from being porous enough to take water-based pigments; without size, absorbing or 'feathering' into the paper takes place. Paper is sized or unsized, the latter is also known as 'waterleaf'.

Vat The tank that holds the mix of water and fibres from which the sheets are made.

Suppliers

Buckram — Art craft supply shops, bookbinder suppliers or:
Russell Bookcrafts, Great North Road, Wyboston, Bedfordshire MK44 3AB
Tel: 0480 405464
Fax: 0480 407105

Cards with cut apertures, greetings card messages, pre-cut picture mounts — Good craft shops or:
Craft Creations Ltd,
Units 1–7 Harpers Yard
Tottenham, London N17 8QA
Tel: 081-885 2655

Caustic soda — Chemists

Cellulose dope — Model shops

Essential oils — Wholefood shops, aromatherapists, branches of Bodyshop

Felts — The Army & Navy Surplus Stores sell old woollen blankets (the plain uncoloured ones are best)

Lacquer spray — Car parts shops

Mould wire — Good hardware shops – look for the plastic-coated wire used to keep flies out of pantries or aluminium mesh.

Vertical blinds — Local curtain shops

Spray-on shoe protector — Shoe or soft furnishing shops

Viscose felts — Local supermarkets

Index

Index

ACKNOWLEDGEMENTS

Thanks are due to: Heather, the editor, and Jon Bouchier, the photographer, for their input that a clear, outside eye can give; my father for his wonderful wordprocessing skills, and my mother for being a five-star granny; all family and friends who have lent me their ears while this book evolved; and, not least, my partner, Stuart, and my children, Bruce and Max, for their patience this summer.